THE AMARANTH

(INDEPENDENT)

A ROYAL AND EXALTED DEGREE

IN THE

RITE OF ADOPTION

WITH APPROPRIATE CEREMONIES

BY

ROBERT MACOY, 33°

SUPREME GRAND PATRON OF THE RITE OF ADOPTION

To which has been added

THE ROYAL MATRONS AND ROYAL PATRONS
ADMINISTRATIVE DEGREE

ADVANCE!

ISBN:978-1-63923-238-3

Printed: June 2022

Cover Art By: Amit Paul

Published and Distributed By:
Lushena Books
607 Country Club Drive, Unit E
Bensenville, IL 60106
www.lushenabooksinc.com/books

ISBN: 978-1-63923-238-3

In Memoriam

THE closing hours of Robert Macoy, the author of this book, were spent in correcting its proof-sheets and arranging the details of its contents. For more than half a century he labored in the field of Masonic literature, and he has left behind him monuments more enduring than marble or bronze. Several generations have come and gone since he first began to impress the beautiful lessons of Truth and Virtue upon the minds of the men with whom he came in contact. His audience was the Masonic world. His words of wisdom were seed-thoughts which have blossomed into a rich and abundant fruitage, and as years roll on in their ceaseless journey, the recurring seasons will add still more to the yield of an ever increasing harvest.

He was a builder, and the great Order of the Eastern Star, as it sheds its brilliant light in the world today, is an evidence of the stability of his work. He foresaw that more than the one degree of the Eastern Star was needed to make the system of degrees in that order complete, and to that end he prepared others, the crowning one being "The Amaranth," which for a time was published with the Eastern Star ritual.

The popularity of The Amaranth, and the desire to establish it as a separate Order, led him to prepare this volume, and with almost his last breath he said, "It is finished." Patiently he labored to correct and revise the ceremonials and to make them most impressive, and when the shadows of the evening gathered about him, he laid aside the busy pen and left to the world as a parting benediction the beautiful ritual of The Amaranth.

How fitting to close a long, busy, and useful life with such a work! How the light seems to gather in celestial brightness about the Crown, and how glitters the sword of Truth as the impressive ceremony of the Accolade is performed!

His work is finished, but its influence will be felt as long as the lessons of The Amaranth are taught; though dead, he will yet speak.

> And when the hour shall come,
> That calls us to his home,
> Those glorious mansions beyond the sky—
> Our Shepherd will bring down
> His Amaranthine crown
> And wreathe our faded brows with victory.

CONTENTS

A FABLE

An Amaranth planted in a garden, near a Rose tree, thus addressed it: "What a lovely flower is the Rose, a favorite alike with gods and with mortals. I envy you your beauty and your perfume." The Rose replied: "I, indeed, dear Amaranth, flourish but for a brief season. If a cruel hand pluck me from my stem, I must perish by an early doom. But *thou art* immortal, and dost never fade, but bloomest forever in renewed youth."

PREFACE

THE intention of the founder and early promoters of the RITE OF ADOPTION was to create a system that would appeal to the highest and noblest aims in life. The tenets set forth in the first degree—the Eastern Star—contain some of the most sublime sentiments known to the human mind—Fidelity, Honor, Virtue, and everything that is pure and elevating. These are taught by facts and symbols, and their beauty is more clear and expressive today than ever before. There are also other and equally beautiful degrees and types, pictures and lessons, that may be impressed on the mind and engraven on the heart.

The RITE OF ADOPTION was never designed to be wholly embodied within the limit of *one* degree; but, like that great institution into whose fraternal organization it was intended to be *adopted*, it should teach its lessons step by step, each advancing ceremony to be higher and more instructive in principle and design. The addition of other and different ceremonies, with beautiful illustrations of Truth, Wisdom, Faith, and Charity, all lovely graces, certainly enhances the value of any association and gives it the right to rank among the great institutions of the world. The Rite of Adoption is designed to be a real and permanent institution.

The Eastern Star degree, as the pioneer, has prepared the way for the presentation, in an intelligent and independent form, of a system whose higher ideas will be commensurate with the scope of its usefulness.

The following letter from Dr. Morris proves that his ideas were in harmony with the plan referred to above:

LA GRANGE, KY., February 22, 1883.

ROBERT MACOY, Esq., *New York:*

R. W. BROTHER: I have given much consideration to your proposal to furnish a series of substantial degrees in the Adoptive Rite. Your plan is admirable. Ever since your establishment of Eastern Star Chapters, in 1868, I have advocated a similar idea as a relief from the *ennui* experienced by the want of variety in chapter work. The one complaint of the ladies is—*the monotony of the endless repetition of one degree.*

Among Masons this same complaint has led to the organization of scores of degrees. The degrees of the Chapter, Council, Commandery, Consistory, etc., all had their origin in the necessity of gratifying the demand for variety. Why should ladies be less favored? It is my opinion that the dullness and lethargy complained of in Eastern Star Chapters can be cured in this way, and only in this.

The list of degrees, whose rituals you will furnish, comprises a variety of thought almost infinite, and will give to the intelligent minds of our sisters subjects of consideration that will enlarge their respect for Freemasonry itself.

I wish you every possible success in disseminating them.

With old time love and esteem,

ROB MORRIS.

The present work has been prepared to complete the original design of the early promoters of the Eastern Star, and to meet the demand for relief from "the monotony of the endless repetition of one degree," as suggested in Dr. Morris's letter.

The Rite of Adoption consists of the following degrees:

1. THE EASTERN STAR, the first or initiatory degree.

2. THE QUEEN OF THE SOUTH, the second degree.

3. THE AMARANTH, the third degree.

The Rituals of these degrees, together with the MATRON's ADMINISTRATIVE degree, have been prepared with great care. The high and noble principles inculcated in them appeal to the better instincts of the human mind.

THE COURT

REVISED RITUAL AND INDEPENDENT ORGANIZATION

The special purpose for introducing the Amaranth degree in its revised and distinct form is to present to the members of the Eastern Star an AD-VANCED and INDEPENDENT organization of the Rite of Adoption, under the title of COURT, thereby intending to afford the best means for exemplifying and appreciating the superior qualities and sublime thoughts inculcated by the previous degrees, and in proper manner supplying a brighter light for those who are desirous of obtaining additional knowledge of the methods of conducting the ceremonials and parliamentary rules of literary, social, and secret associations.

The SUPREME COUNCIL of the Rite of Adoption of the World, was established June 14, 1873, of which the subscriber was elected and installed Supreme Patron, and Bro. Rob Morris, Supreme Recorder, which office he held until the time of his death.

The following official authority, and fulfillment of the service, relates to the Amaranth degree.

OFFICE OF THE SUPREME PATRON, ADOPTIVE RITE,
LA GRANGE, KY., 29 April, 1875.

PROFESSOR ANDRES CASSARD, *New York:*

ILLUSTRIOUS BRO.: Reposing implicit confidence in your zeal, knowledge, and discretion, I hereby em-

power and request you to install the Very Illustrious
ROBERT MACOY as my successor in the position of
Supreme Patron of the World, Adoptive Rite.
Herein make report of your proceedings to me.

ROB MORRIS, [Seal.]

Supreme Patron, Adoptive Rite.

NEW YORK, May 3, 1875.

In compliance with the above request, I installed
Ill. Bro. Robert Macoy as Supreme Patron of the
Adoptive Rite.

ANDRES CASSARD.

———

Courteously,

ROBERT MACOY

———

FLORAL SYMBOLIC MEANING OF THE AMARANTH

IN floral language the most poetical of all flowers
is the AMARANTH, christened by the Greeks *"Never-
Fading."* Because of the lasting nature of its
bloom, it has been selected as the SYMBOL OF
IMMORTALITY, and as such has ever been associated with the sublime idea of a future life. The
possession of its earliest blossoms afforded the belief that the soul would enjoy eternal rest in the
realms of the Celestial Home.

In Portugal and other warm climates, the people adorn the
churches at Christmas time with the Amaranth, as an emblem of
that immortality which their faith bids them look forward to.
To the lover the gift of its flower is ever a symbol of undying
love.

GRAND STANDARD

PUBLISHERS' FOREWORD

THE INITIATORY WORK HAS NOT BEEN CHANGED

THOSE jurisdictions which use *only* the Initiatory Ceremony, working this as a degree of the Eastern Star *Chapter* and do not use the *Court* Opening and Closing Ceremonies, will find no changes from the previous editions.

However, for the many jurisdictions which use the entire *Amaranth Ritual,* working this as a degree of the Adoptive Rite system, and not of the Chapter, will welcome, we believe, the inclusion of the work and duties of the Marshals. These two officers have been included in the list of officers and their respective stations shown in previous editions but, through oversight, the work for them was omitted.

This edition in no way deviates from the true Amaranth ritual as compiled by the venerable Robert Macoy as his last contribution to the Order he so loved. Nor will the previous Macoy editions be obsolete.

The book has been set in larger and more readable type and, while we have retained the early illustrations which are both instructive and interesting, we have given more explicit diagrams for marching. Sketchy instructions which have appeared in the earlier editions have been put into dialogue in order that the commands given the various officers be more uniform and dignified.

Paraphernalia for a Court, instructions for Opening and marching, as well as preliminary preparations and instructions for conferring the degree, have been given.

Those Grand Courts authorizing an Associate Patron and a Chaplain will find the work and duties for these optional officers also included. The material on optional officers has been set in italics so that no confusion will arise and these sections may be omitted if such officers are not authorized by your Grand Court.

Finally, the material has been so organized and arranged that quick reference to any section is an easy matter by consulting the Contents page following this Foreword.

The Publishers sincerely trust that the arrangement of this edition will contribute to a still more dignified and efficient rendition of the work.

THE PUBLISHERS

August, 1952

INTRODUCTION

IDEAL INSTITUTIONS are those organizations which, moved by a superior and creative inspiration, take the lead in the moral culture and civilization of the nations, and preside over their spiritual and intellectual development.

ACTUAL INSTITUTIONS are those organizations which spring from some thought, relation or inspiration to produce and establish a complete and perfect achievement; an existing and acting association for some benevolent, religious, political or social purpose; a genuine and positive reality, laboring to accomplish mutual and actual results.

In the earlier periods of the world, the wisest and best of men withdrew from the imperfections of the exterior society, and in their secret temples sought to sound the mysterious systems of God, Nature, and the Soul, and to live out their idea of a true life. The Mysteries of Egypt, of Eleusis, of the Cabiri, and those of India and of the North of Europe, had a widely extended influence; and so important were they, that an investigation of them is necessary, if we would have an accurate view of the Theology, Philosophy, Science, and Ethics of the past times.

It was a part of the mission of these institutions in general, to elevate the tone of public and private morals, and to cause to be realized, in all the arrangements of life, a diviner sentiment of JUSTICE, a truer ideal of CHARITY, and more enlightened notions regarding our relations with each other.

For many years there was no intelligent expression of this social idea in which women, however educated or talented, could join. They are debarred by their sex from initiation into Freemasonry, which is the embodiment of social union, and it was not until the Eastern Star or Rite of Adoption was established, that any approach was made to bring them even within the outer courts of the Mystic Temple. This happily has been done, and has proved successful.

There is and always will be a need of institutions similar and of cognate qualities to our ADOPTIVE RITE, where a higher Ideal of Life may be sought after and recognized than has yet been found in the ordinary fraternal organizations of the day—institutions which will combine the scattered elements of society, arm itself against the selfish tendencies of the race, give humanity faith in virtue and confidence in each other, and reveal to the world a Divine Ideal.

HISTORICAL BACKGROUND

The first organizations, claiming to imitate Freemasonry in form, ceremony, and usefulness, to which females were admitted to membership, were established in France, about the year 1730. They were called *"Loges d'Adoption,"* or "ADOPTIVE LODGES," because every Lodge of Adoption was required to be under the guardianship of some regular Masonic Lodge.

By the term *Adoptive Masonry* (or *Rite of Adoption*) is implied that system of forms, ceremonies, and lectures which is communicated to certain classes of ladies, who, from their relationship by blood or marriage to Master Masons in good standing, are entitled to the respect and attention of the Fraternity. The ladies were *adopted* into the Masonic communion, to enable them to express their wishes and give satisfactory evidence of their claims, in a manner that no stranger to the Masonic family could.

On June 10, 1774, the Grand Orient (Grand Lodge) of France issued an edict by which it assumed the control of Lodges of Adoption. Rules and regulations were provided for the government of these Lodges of Adoption, one of which was that men, except regular Freemasons, should not be permitted to attend them and that each Lodge of Adoption should be placed under the charge of some regularly constituted Masonic Lodge.

It will thus be seen that the present system is properly called the "RITE OF ADOPTION," because the same character of organization received recognition by regular Masonic bodies in France, Germany, Italy, and other countries; and, under the guardianship of a Masonic Lodge, these bodies may be adopted into the family of the Fraternity, and become one of its important and useful branches.

The original Royal and Exalted Order of the Amaranth was created by CHRISTINA, Queen of Sweden, A.D. 1653, to honor the LADY AMARANTA, a woman of rare beauty, modesty, and charity, who was attached to the Court of Sweden. For a long time this knightly Order was immensely popular in Europe, and the most distinguished ladies and gentlemen considered themselves honored by being made members of it.

The theory of Knighthood and its Orders, as applied to the citizens of a republican form of government, is in some respects different from that applied to the subjects of a monarchical state. This is seen in the witty observation of James I., King of England, when asked by his nurse to make her son a gentleman, he replied: "I will make him a Baronet, but no power on earth can make him a gentleman." In this declaration the King expressed the whole subject, as understood in his day. But in America, where the *people* are sovereigns, all are born equal, and MERIT is the elevating standard of true nobility. In introducing the Amaranthine Order, Robert Macoy's purpose, therefore, was to inquire only for noble *deeds*, knowing and caring nothing for noble *birth*.

PURPOSES AND TEACHINGS OF THE DEGREE

The present *independent* form of the Royal and Exalted degree of the Amaranth is adapted to the demands of those who are seeking light and *Advancement*. It is made to form the apex of the Rite of Adoption, and to establish a COURT OF HONOR, wherein the highest grade of instruction, culture, and usefulness may be imparted, in symbolical guise, to the *Advanced* members of the Rite.

The teachings of the degree are meant to impress upon us our duty to God, to country, and to one another that we may live in peace and harmony with our fellowmen, being charitable in thoughts as well as in our deeds; that by following the virtues of Truth, Faith, Wisdom and Charity, we may so exercise an influence for good upon those we meet that it may truly be said of us when we lay down our tools of labor that the world is a little better for our having lived in it.

This is the first law to be established in friendship, that we neither ask of others that which is dishonorable, nor ourselves do wrong when asked.

It was established for the admission and benefit of man and woman upon a perfect equality. It is CHARITABLE and BENEVOLENT to the extent of its opportunities and ability. It seeks to unfold the divine possibilities which are resident in every human soul, and affords an opportunity for woman to become conversant with the usages of societies and fit herself for positions of honor, trust, and responsibility.

LANDMARKS OF THE RITE

1. The Eastern Star is the basis of the Degrees of the Rite of Adoption; the name and character of the Rite are unchangeable.

2. Its lessons are Scriptural, its teachings are moral, and its purposes are beneficent.

3. A belief in the existence of a Supreme Being, who will punish the violation of a solemn pledge.

4. Its obligations are based upon the honor of the female sex who obtain its ceremonies, and are framed upon the principle that whatever benefits are due by the Masonic Fraternity *to* the wives, mothers, widows, daughters, and sisters of Masons, corresponding benefits are due *from* them to the brotherhood.

5. The modes of recognition, which are the peculiar secrets of the Rite, cannot, without destroying the foundation of the system, be changed.

6. That a covenant of secrecy, voluntarily assumed, is perpetual; from the force of such obligation there is no release.

7. The control of this degree lies in the bodies styled the Supreme Council, or the Grand Court of the State of ...., of the Adoptive Rite, or in the prerogatives of the Supreme Patron, or executive officer, when the Supreme Council or Grand Court is not in session.

8. That the ballot for candidates for membership must be unanimous, and be kept inviolably secret.

9. The right of every Court to be the judge of who shall be admitted to its membership, and to select its own officers; but in no case can the ceremonies of the Rite be conferred unless a Master Mason, in good standing in the Masonic Fraternity, and a member of the Court, presides.

10. Every member is amenable to the laws and regulations of the Rite, and may be tried for offenses, though permanently or temporarily residing within the jurisdiction of another Court.

11. The right of every member to appeal from the decision of a subordinate Court to the Grand Court or Supreme Council, the Grand Matron or Supreme Patron.

12. The prerogative of the Supreme or Grand

Patron to preside over every assembly of the Rite wherever he may visit, and to grant Charters for the formation of new Courts within the territorial jurisdiction.

13. That every Court has the right to dispense the light of the Adoptive Rite, and to administer its own private affairs.

14. Every Court should elect and install its officers annually.

15. The right of every member to visit and sit in every regular Court, except when such visitor may disturb the harmony or interrupt the business of the Court.

GENERAL REGULATIONS

TITLE

This organization shall be known as "THE RITE OF ADOPTION OF THE WORLD," and shall consist of the degrees of the Eastern Star, the Queen of the South, and the Amaranth.

GOVERNMENT AND AUTHORITY

The government of the Rite is vested in the Supreme Council, Grand Courts, and Subordinate Courts.

SUPREME COUNCIL

THE SUPREME COUNCIL, by the inherent authority of possession and right of eminent domain, has exclusive power to establish Courts in jurisdictions, domestic and foreign, where no Grand Court of the Rite exists; to establish a uniform system of work and lectures; has jurisdiction over all subjects of legislation and appellate powers to hear and decide all questions of law and equity that may be brought before it, and to do each and everything appertaining to the good and perpetuity of the Rite, in accordance with its Constitution.

GRAND COURT—HOW CONSTITUTED

Three or more Subordinate Courts chartered by authority of the Supreme Court, in any state, country or territory in which there is no Grand Court of the Rite of Adoption, may form a Grand Court by delegates duly appointed, and having the approval of the Supreme Court or the Supreme Patron.

Each Grand Court shall have exclusive authority to constitute new Courts within its jurisdiction, and to ordain and prescribe regulations for their government: *Provided*, that they are not in conflict with the Constitution of the Supreme Council.

SUBORDINATE COURT

A Subordinate Court has authority for action:

1. In all matters of discipline involving inquiry into misconduct, and trial and punishment for the same; provided, that in all cases an appeal to the Grand Court or Grand Matron shall be allowed.

2. In all appropriations of the funds of the Court.

3. In the free choice and selection of its officers and members.

4. In the disposition of its own property, except its charter, books of record and accounts. These, of right, belong to the Grand Court or Supreme Council.

MEETINGS

The meetings of the Court are *Regular* or *Special.*

The *Regular* meetings are those enjoined by the by-laws, and may be held weekly, semi-monthly, or monthly, at the choice of the members expressed in the by-laws.

The *Special* meetings are those summoned at the will of the Royal Matron, or, in her absence, by the Associate Matron, upon any proper emergency.

No meeting, either *Regular* or *Special,* can be lawfully held unless the Charter be present.

No business is proper at a *Special* meeting, except such as shall be stated in the call.

The place of meeting may be in a hall or private apartment. It must be sufficiently secluded to insure secrecy. A contiguous apartment for the preparation of candidates, the reception of visitors, etc., is essential.

QUORUM FOR BUSINESS

A meeting of the Court, for any business except conferring the degree, may be opened and held by seven members, the Royal Matron or Associate Matron being one. The number proper to confer the degree must be at least fourteen, of which the Royal Patron shall be one.

USE OF THE GAVEL

One blow (*) of the gavel calls the Court to order; establishes a decision; or seats the Court; two blows (**) call up the officers; three blows (***) call up everyone in the room.

MEMBERSHIP

The lawful recipients of the degree of the Amaranth are the wives, mothers, widows, daughters, or sisters of affiliated Master Masons, and Master Masons, who have previously received the Eastern Star degree.

The requisite qualifications for initiation and membership are good moral character, ability to gain a livelihood or some visible means of support.

No person can be an active member of more than one Court at the same time, nor shall any member be permitted to withdraw from a Court until all dues and other indebtedness to the same are paid or remitted.

FORFEITURE OF MEMBERSHIP

The membership of a Sister is forfeited:

1. By suspension for non-payment of dues.
2. By expulsion for just cause.
3. By dismission.

Restoration by the Court will remove causes 1 and 2. Affiliation will remove cause 3.

The membership of a Brother is forfeited:

1. By suspension, explusion, or dimission from the Masonic Lodge of which he was a member.
2. By suspension or expulsion from the Court.
3. By dimission.

Restoration by the Lodge will remove cause 1; restoration by the Court will remove cause 2. Affiliation will remove cause 3.

APPLICATION FOR DIMIT

To the Royal Matron, Officers and Members of .....
Court No. .... of the State of ......:
The undersigned, now a member of this Court, and
having paid all known dues and assessments, respect-
fully requests a Dimit from the Court.
(Signed) ....
Date ....

DIMIT

Dolce nella Memoria—"Sweet in Memory"
To the Members of the RITE OF ADOPTION, wherever
dispersed, this Certificate of Withdrawal certifies:
That Sister (*brother*) ...., whose name appears
in the margin of this DIMIT, was a member of ......
Court No. ...., holden at ......, State of ......, in
good standing, and having complied with all the legal
requirements of this Court, we do cordially recommend
her (*him*) to the affectionate regard and protection of
all true members of the Rite wherever dispersed.
In testimony whereof, we have caused this DIMIT to
be signed by the Royal Matron and Royal Patron, and
the seal of the Court to be attached, this ... day of
......, 19.....

(SEAL) ....R. M.
.... Secretary ....R. P.

PETITIONS

Proposals for membership must be made by a member of the Court who must give the name, residence, age, occupation, and name and number of the Eastern Star Chapter of the applicant. One or more references are required. The proposer of candidates should be careful to propose only those persons as will conform to the rules and precepts of the Order, making sure that they are in good standing in their Eastern Star Chapter, that they are of good moral character, industrious, temperate, and exempt from infirmities that would render them liable to become dependent upon the Court.

Petitions must be presented at a *Regular* meeting and be referred to a committee of three members for investigation. The report of the committee and election by ballot must not take place before the next *Regular* meeting. Conferring the degree may take place at a Special meeting, but the petition cannot be offered or voted upon except at a Regular meeting.

FORM OF PETITION FOR MEMBERSHIP

Date ....

To the Royal Matron, Officers and Members of .....
Court No. ...., of the State of ......:

The undersigned respectfully solicits the honor of ADVANCEMENT into the Royal and Exalted Degree of the Amaranth in your Court.

Name ....Age........
Residence ....
Occupation ....
I am a member in good standing of ...... Chapter No.
...., State of ...... I am in good health and have no
infirmities except ....

If the prayer of this petition shall be granted, I pledge
my honor that I will, in all respects, conform to the requirements of your Court, and be subject to the Constitution of the Supreme Court, and the Rules and Regulations of the Grand Court.

(Signed) ....
Proposed by ....
References ....
....

NOTE.—The petition having been presented, received,
and referred to the committee, it is the property of the
Court and becomes a part of the records regardless of
the outcome of the ballot, and cannot be withdrawn, except for constitutional irregularity.

AFFILIATION

A petition for affiliation should be accompanied
with a dimit, presented at a regular meeting of the
Court, and referred to a committee of three, and is
subject to the same course of inquiry as required
upon propositions for initiations. If the applicant
shall be elected, a dimit from the former Court must
be presented to the Court before the petitioner can
be permitted to sign the by-laws and complete
membership.

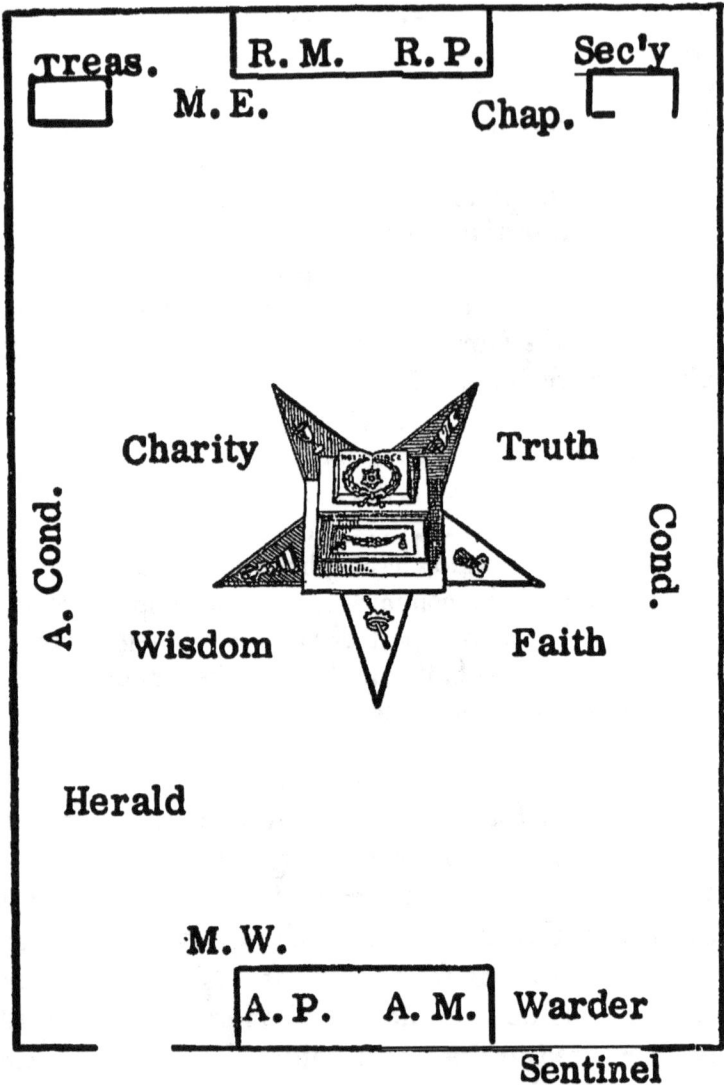

Treas.   R. M.   R. P.   Sec'y
          M. E.   Chap.

A. Cond.   Charity   Truth   Cond.

                Wisdom   Faith

Herald

·M. W.

          A. P.   A. M.   Warder
                              Sentinel

OFFICERS' STATIONS

OFFICERS AND THEIR STATIONS

1. ROYAL MATRON, in the East.
2. ROYAL PATRON, in the East, at the left of the R. M.
3. ASSOCIATE MATRON, in the West.
4. ASSOCIATE PATRON, *in the West, at the left of the of the A. M.*
5. TREASURER, in the East, to the right of the R. M.
6. SECRETARY, in the East, to the left of the R. P.
7. CONDUCTRESS, in the South.
8. ASSOCIATE CONDUCTRESS, in the North.
9. CHAPLAIN, *at the foot of the dais in the East, to the left of the R. P.*
10. TRUTH, at the Southeast corner of the Altar, facing East.
11. FAITH, at the Southwest corner of the Altar, facing East.
12. WISDOM, at the Northwest corner of the Altar, facing East.
13. CHARITY, at the Northeast corner of the Altar, facing East.
14. HERALD, in the West, to the left and in front of the A. M.
15. MARSHAL IN THE EAST, at the foot of the dais in the East, to the right of the R. M.
16. MARSHAL IN THE WEST, to the right, and behind, the Herald in the West.
17. WARDER, inside the door.
18. SENTINEL, outside the door.

NOTE: *The Associate Patron and Chaplain are optional officers, depending on the regulation of your Grand Court.*

OFFICERS' JEWELS

Officers will be distinguished by their jewels in the form of a five-pointed star, with appropriate emblem of office in the center, and suspended from the sash, over the left breast, as follows:

1. ROYAL MATRON, Star with Sword and Royal Crown.
2. ROYAL PATRON, Star, with Fasces, surmounted by an antique Lamp, lighted, and Balance.
3. ASSOCIATE MATRON, Star, with Hands holding Wreath.
4. ASSOCIATE PATRON, same as R. P.
5. TREASURER, Star, with Crossed Keys.
6. SECRETARY, Star, with Crossed Pens.
7. CONDUCTRESS, Star, with Scroll and Baton.
8. ASSOCIATE CONDUCTRESS, Star, with Baton.
9. CHAPLAIN, Star, with open Bible.
10. TRUTH, Star, with Angel.
11. FAITH, Star, with Female Figure and Cross.
12. WISDOM, Star, with figure Minerva and an owl.
13. CHARITY, Star, with Female Figure and Children.
14. HERALD, Star, with Standard.
15. MARSHAL IN THE EAST, Star, with Crossed Batons.
16. MARSHAL IN THE WEST, Star, with Crossed Batons.
17. WARDER, Star, with Flying Dove.
18. SENTINEL, Star, with Crossed Swords.

ROYAL MATRON   ASSOCIATE MATRON

ROYAL PATRON

CONDUCTRESS   ASSOCIATE CONDUCTRESS

SECRETARY   TREASURER

CHARITY   TRUTH

WISDOM   FAITH

HERALD
MARSHALS

CHAPLAIN

WARDER   SENTINEL

OFFICERS' REGALIA

The ROYAL MATRON will wear a sash, or scarf, of scarlet silk velvet, three or four inches wide, edged with gold silk braid and trimmed with gold silk fringe; embroidered with vine work in gold silk; on the shoulder, a five-pointed silk Star in the five colors; at the crossing, a golden rosette, from which is suspended two gold tassels. The sash is to be worn from the left shoulder to the right and the jewel of office is to be pinned on the sash over the left breast.

TRUTH, FAITH, WISDOM, and CHARITY will wear Blue, Yellow, White, and Green silk moire ribbon sashes, respectively; four inches wide, with gold rosette and two tassels at the crossing; trimmed with gold silk fringe at the ends of sash.

OTHER OFFICERS wear four inch wide Red silk moire ribbon sashes, trimmed as above.

The GRAND ROYAL MATRON'S sash is the same as for the Royal Matron, except it is embroidered in gold BULLION and trimmed with gold BULLION fringe along one side and on the ends; the letters: G.R.M. and the year of holding office are embroidered on the sash between the five-colored silk Star on the shoulder and the top of the vine work.

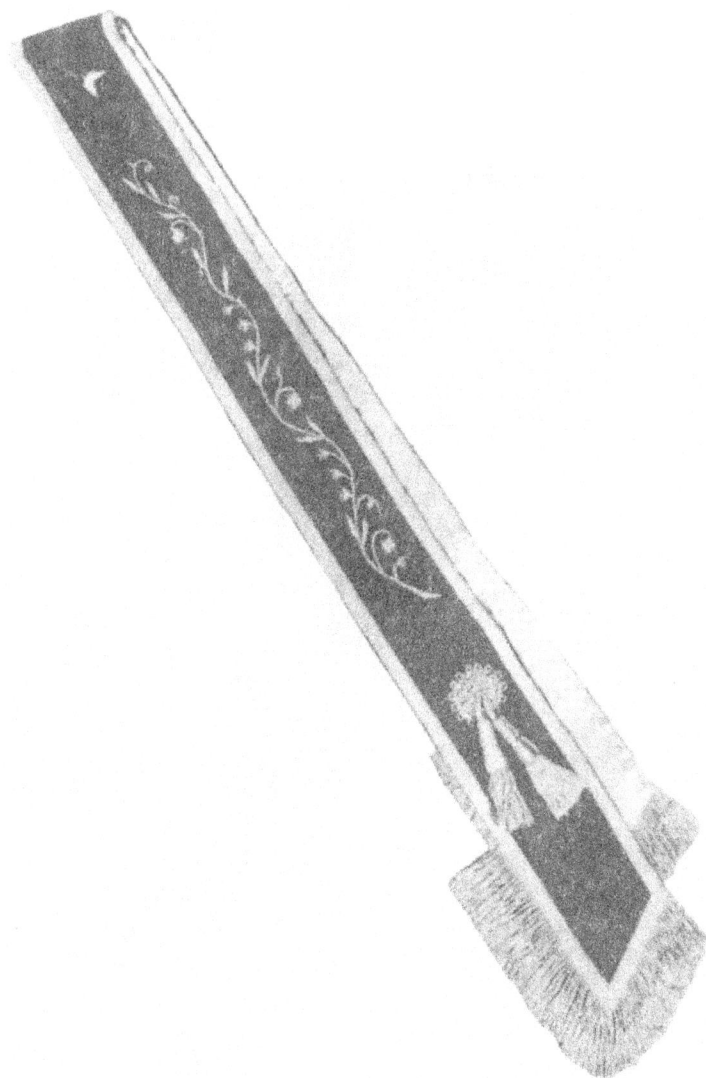

OFFICER'S SASH

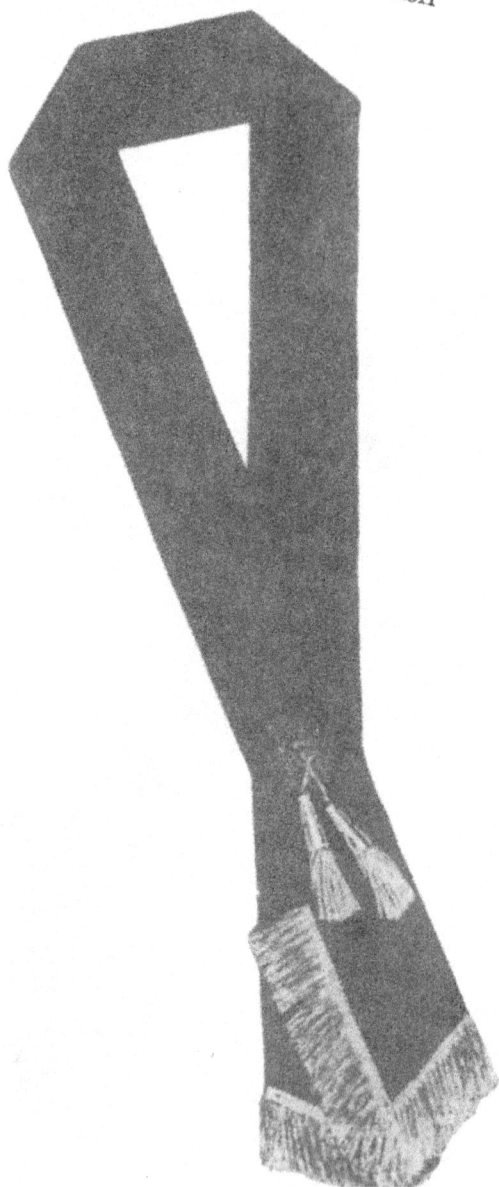

BADGE OF THE RITE

The badge of the Rite is of yellow metal (usually gold), circular. In the center, a fasces, the crest an antique lamp, lighted, within a wreath of Amaranth, bound with white ribbon on which is the motto, *"Dolce nella Memoria";* supported by the figures, Plenty and Charity. On the outer circle, the letters: AMARANTUS, laid upon and interwoven through the Eastern Star emblem.

PARAPHERNALIA FOR A COURT

1. Altar in the center of the room.
2. Holy Bible for the Altar.
3. Wreath of artificial Amaranth leaves for the open Bible. May be taken to the West for coronation and then returned.
4. Eastern Star Floor Carpet.
5. Pedestals and Chairs in the East and West.
6. Gavels for Royal Matron and Associate Matron.
7. Crown and Sword for the Royal Matron.
8. Altar and Pedestal Covers.
9. Ballot Box with white balls and black cubes, or balls.
10. Basin for ceremony of ablution.
11. Patens for salt and small pieces of bread, to be covered with a white napkin.
12. Seal Press.
13. U.S. Flag.

14. Grand Standard of the Rite which should be about 25 x 36 inches; white, on which is embroidered or painted the badge of the Amaranth degree; An All-Seeing-Eye; a descending Dove with Olive Branch in its beak; trimmed with gold braid and fringe; suspended from a cross bar attached to a pole.

15. Small banners, approximately 18 x 24 inches for TRUTH, FAITH, WISDOM, and CHARITY. These may all be scarlet or Blue, Yellow, White, and Green, respectively; embroidered or painted with the station name and figures as follows:

   TRUTH—Angel

   FAITH—Female Figure and Cross

   WISDOM—Minerva figure and an Owl

   CHARITY—Female Figure and Children

   Trimmed with gold braid and suspended from cross bars attached to poles.

16. Six Stands, or holders, for Flag, Standard (2), Station Banners (4).

BALLOTING

R. M.—Honored Associate Conductress.

A. COND.—Royal Matron.

R. M.—Prepare the ballot box.

(A. C. should have seen that the ballot box, with sufficient white balls and black cubes, was placed beneath her chair before the meeting opened. She looks to see that there are balls and cubes in the box and then reports):

A. COND.—Royal Matron, the ballot box is prepared.

R. M.—Present the ballot box for inspection.

(A. C. carries the box by way of the West to the East and R. M. and R. P. inspect it. R. P. holds the box while R. M. says):

R. M.—Honored Ladies and Sir Knights of .... Court, we are about to ballot on the petition of .... for membership in this Court. Those in favor of granting the prayer of the petitioner will cast a white ball, and those opposed, a black cube.

(R. M. and R. P. will then cast their ballots)

R. M.—Honored Associate Conductress, carry the ballot box to the Associate Matron *(and Associate Patron)* in the West for her *(their)* ballot(s) and then place it upon the Altar.

44

(A. C. complies with the order)

R. M.—The other officers and members will proceed, in order, to ballot.

(When all have voted):

R. M.—All having balloted, I declare the ballot closed. Honored Associate Conductress, carry the ballot box to the West and then to the East for inspection.

(After the box has been examined by the A. M., and the Matron finding one rejecting ballot therein, she may, without remark, order a second ballot, to correct a possible mistake. If, however, two or more rejecting ballots are found in the box, a second ballot should not be ordered. If there are no rejecting ballots on the first ballot, the Matron will ask):

R. M.—Honored Associate Matron, how is the ballot in the West?

A. M.—The ballot is clear in the West, Royal Matron.

R. M.—Royal Patron, how is the ballot in the East?

R. P.—The ballot is clear in the East, Royal Matron.

R. M.—The ballot being clear in the West and in the East, I have the pleasure to inform you that .... *(giving name)*—has been elected to become a member of this Court.*

If rejecting ballots appear in the ballot-box, the Associate Matron, after being asked, will say:

A. M.—The ballot is not clear in the West, Royal Matron.

R. M.—The ballot not being clear in the East, it is my duty to announce the petition of . . . . is rejected.

INSTRUCTIONS FOR OPENING
AND MARCHING

Before the Court is opened the Flag should be placed at the Herald's station and the Grand Standard placed in the East. The banners for Truth, Faith, Wisdom and Charity should be placed behind the chairs of these respective stations. The Amaranthine wreath should be placed on the closed Bible on the Altar.

If there is to be balloting, the Associate Conductress will see that the ballot box with sufficient white balls and black cubes is placed beneath her chair before the Court opens.

The Royal Patron, Associate Patron (if this office is authorized by your Grand Court) and the Musician will be at their respective stations, as will the Associate Conductress until she is instructed to invite the Royal Matron and the other officers in. After she has done so, she will take her position in the line of march as follows:

THE EAST

A. COND..		COND.
TREAS.		SEC.
CHARITY		TRUTH
WISDOM		FAITH
HERALD		WARDER

A. M. R. M.
MARSHAL   MARSHAL

47

DIAGRAM 1

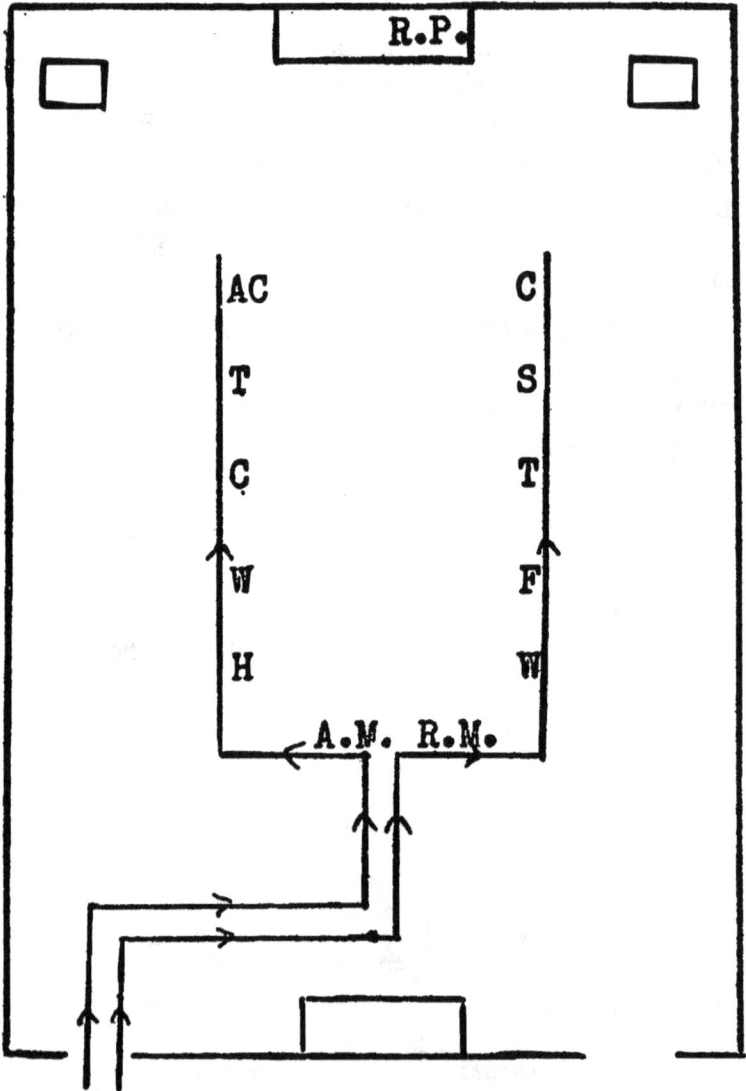

Conductresses leading, Officers march to positions as shown in Diagram 1. By the time the Conductresses have reached the foot of the throne all the officers are in position and all officers salute the Royal Patron with the public sign of salutation, the Royal Patron returning the salute.

> *NOTE: If opened as a* Court, *and not as a* Chapter, *the Marshals will lead the Officers into the room and take ·positions at the right and left of Associate Matron's station (see line up on page 47), leaving enough room for the other Officers to pass in front of them to positions as indicated in DIAGRAM 1. Marshals may carry batons or officers' rods.*

> *If Chaplain is used, she will follow the Warder.*

> *When Officers resume their stations, Marshals move last.*

Officers will observe square corners when marching and should keep abreast of the officer in the opposite line of march; keep approximately three steps apart when marching and also when standing in line at the finish of the opening march.

DIAGRAM 2

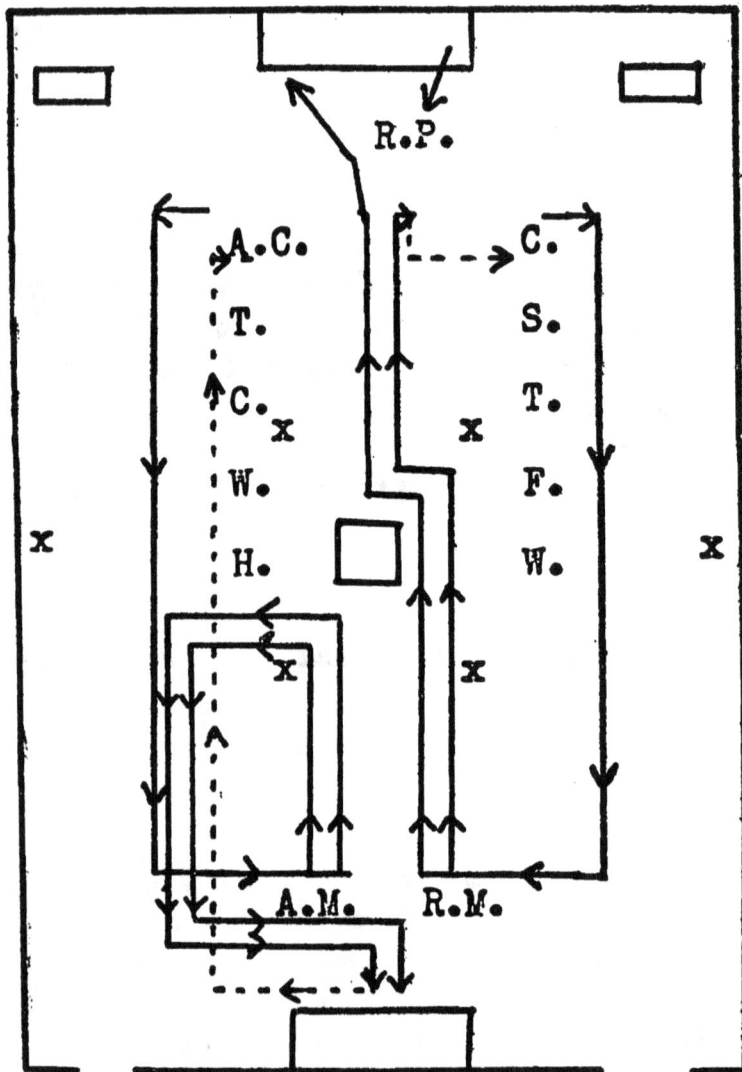

R.P.

A.C.
T.
C.   x
W.
H.

C.
S.
T.
F.
W.

x

x

x

x

x

A.M.   R.M.

The Conductresses turn out, take one step South and North, respectively, then march directly West opposite the R. M. and A. M., turn towards center. As the Conductresses approach them, the R. M. and A. M. face South and North, respectively. When the Conductresses reach these officers, all face East and march four abreast simultaneously. R. M. and Cond. continue East as indicated in diagram 2. A. M. and A. C. march East beyond the chair of Wisdom, turn North, turn West, turn South to A. M.'s station.

The Conductresses return to their places in the line of march as indicated by the dotted lines in the diagram.

All officers, when commanded to do so, will reach their stations by the most direct route, making square corners whenever turning.

If Marshals are used, they wait until all other Officers have reached their respective stations before assuming theirs.

OPENING CEREMONY

The time appointed in the By-laws, or named in the special notice, having arrived, all the officers will retire to the anteroom with exception of the Royal Patron, Associate Conductress, Musician (and Associate Patron, if this office is filled). These officers will assume their respective stations. The Royal Patron will call the Court to order with one blow of the gavel (*).

R. P.—Honored Ladies and Sir Knights, ... Court No. ..... is about to be opened. If there be any present who are not entitled to remain, they will please retire.

R. P.—Honored Associate Conductress,[1] invite the Royal Matron and the other officers to enter the Court room.

MUSIC

(*A. C. retires and returns with the officers who enter in two lines, as per preceding Diagram 1.*)

R. P.—*** (*calls up the entire room*)

(*After officers are in line as in Diagram 1 and have saluted the R. P.*):

R. P.—Honored Conductress and Associate Conductress, escort the Royal Matron and Associate Matron to their respective stations, on the throne and in the West.

---

[1] *The Royal Matron and Royal Patron should pause after addressing an officer to give such officer time to rise and respond.*

(See Diagram 2. R. P. descends to meet the R. M. and escorts her to the throne. After Conductresses have returned to their places in the line):

R. P.—Royal Matron, we welcome you with a cordial greeting, and request you to open this Court according to the forms and ceremonies of the Rite *(hands her the gavel).*

R. M.—The officers will take their respective stations, and assist in the active duties of the Court.

(When all officers are at their stations):

R. M.—Attention, you will unite with me in pledging allegiance to our country's flag.

(Marshal in the East ascends the throne, takes the flag and all officers step down on the floor. All place right hand over left breast.)

ALL—I pledge allegiance to the Flag of, *etc.*

(All unite in singing any appropriate patriotic song.)

R. M.—* *(seats the Court)*

M. in E.—*(replaces the flag in its holder on the throne and takes her seat)*

R. M.—Honored Warder.

WAR.—Royal Matron.[1]

R. M.—We are about to open .... Court No. ...... for the transaction of business; inform the Sentinel and direct him to use proper vigilance in protecting us from interruption.

WAR.—(*gives three raps* * * * *which are answered by* * * * *from the Sentinel.. Warder opens the door.*) Sir Knight Sentinel, we are about to open ...... Court and you are directed to use proper vigilance in protecting us from interruption.

WAR.—Your order has been obeyed, Royal Matron.

R. M.—Honored Associate Matron.

A. M.—Royal Matron.

R. M.—Are all present entitled to the privileges of the degree?

A. M.—I will ascertain and report. Honored Conductress, ascertain and report if all present are entitled to the privileges of the degree.

(*If there be a large gathering, the R. M. may ask the Associate Conductress to assist the Conductress in taking up the password. The Conductresses will pass down the North and South sides of the room, taking the password and grip from any with whom they are not acquainted or certain. If there be any present who cannot give the password and grip, the Conductresses will so report to the A. M. and if she cannot vouch for*

---

[1] *Officers will rise and respond when addressed, and remain standing until they have performed the duty requested from the E6K.*

*them, she will report to the R. M. as follows: A. M.—
"Royal Matron, an Honored Lady without the password and grip." If the R. M. or none in the Court can
vouch for such person, the R. M. will immediately
appoint an investigating committee who will retire
with such person, or persons, not vouched for, under
escort of the Marshal in the East.)*

COND.—Honored Associate Matron, all present
are entitled to the privileges of the degree.

A. M.—All present are entitled to the privileges
of the degree, Royal Matron.

R. M.—I am pleased to extend a hearty welcome
to all. Honored Warder, how are we protected?

WAR.—By a brother Sir Knight, faithful and
vigilant, at the entrance to the Court room.

R. M.—Inform us as to your station and duties.

WAR.—My station is at the portals of the Court
room. My duty is to announce all persons duly
vouched for seeking admission, so that none may
enter our Court but those who are entitled to enjoy
the privileges of the degree, and to perform such
other duties as may best promote the interests of
the Court.

R. M.—Where is our Honored Lady Charity stationed?

WAR.—At the Northeast corner of the altar,
Royal Matron.

R. M.—Honored Lady Charity, what are your
duties?

CHARITY—To demonstrate that Charity, which is the bond of perfection, is kind and just, long suffering, tender and forgiving; also to assist in the benevolent works of the Court.

R. M.—Where is our Honored Lady Wisdom stationed?

CHARITY—At the Northwest corner of the altar, Royal Matron.

R. M.—Honored Lady Wisdom, what are your duties?

WISDOM—To explain the greatness and majesty of Wisdom, whose ways are ways of pleasantness and whose paths are peace, and to assist the Court in enlarging its power to do good.

R. M.—Where is our Honored Lady Faith stationed?

WISDOM—At the Southwest corner of the altar, Royal Matron.

R. M.—Honored Lady Faith, what are your duties?

FAITH—To teach the importance of abiding faith in God, and confidence in our fellow creatures, and to aid the Court in performing deeds of kindness.

R. M.—Where is our Honored Lady Truth stationed?

FAITH—At the Southeast corner of the altar, Royal Matron.

R. M.—Honored Lady Truth, what are your duties?

TRUTH—To inculcate the force and grandeur of truth, which is eternal, all powerful, and fearless, and to assist the Court in maintaining equal justice to all.

R. M.—Where is our Honored Herald stationed?

TRUTH—In the West in front, and at the left hand of the Honored Associate Matron, Royal Matron.

R. M.—Honored Herald, what are your duties?

HERALD—To proclaim the God-like attribute Mercy, gentle and loving in all its acts, with tenderness watching over the distressed; to display the Standard of the Rite, and perform such other duties as may be required by the Court.

R. M.—Where is the Honored Marshal in the West stationed?

HERALD—At the left and in front of the Honored Associate Matron in the West, Royal Matron.

R. M.—Honored Marshal in the West, what are your duties?

M. in W.—To assist in the formation of processions and escort work, and to perform such other duties as occasion may require.

R. M.—Where is the Honored Marshal in the East stationed?

M. in W.—*In front of the throne, at the right of the Royal Matron.*

R. M.—*Honored Marshal in the East, what are your duties?*

M. in E.—*To assist in the formation of processions; display the Flag of our Country; act as an escort to the Royal Matron and to perform such other duties as may be required.*

R. M.—*Where is the Honored Chaplain stationed?*[1]

M. in E.—*In front of the throne, at the left of the Royal Patron.*

R. M.—*Honored Chaplain, what are your duties?*

CHAP.—*To lead in the devotional exercises of the Court when asked to do so by the Royal Patron, and have a watchful care over the spiritual needs of the members.*

R. M.—Where is the Honored Associate Conductress stationed?

M. in E. *or* CHAP.—In the North, Royal Matron.

R. M.—Honored Associate Conductress, what are your duties?

A. C.—To perform the constitutional requirements of my office, prepare candidates for the de-

---

[1] *Material set in italics is optional depending on whether or not these officers are used.*

gree of this Court, and assist the Honored Conductress in the discharge of the duties of her office.

R. M.—Where is the Honored Conductress stationed?

A. C.—In the South, Royal Matron.

R. M.—Honored Conductress, what are your duties?

COND.—To assist the officers of the Court in the performance of their duties, to see that none are present but those who are entitled to the privileges of the Court, receive and conduct candidates through the degree of the Court, and aid in extending the welcome due to visitors.

R. M.—Where is the Honored Treasurer stationed?

COND.—At the Place of Finance, in the Northeast, Royal Matron.

R. M.—Honored Treasurer, what are your duties?

TREAS.—To receive from the Secretary the monies of the Court, keep correct accounts of its financial affairs, and pay all bills ordered by the Court and approved by the Royal Matron.

R. M.—Where is the Honored Secretary stationed?

TREAS.—At the Place of Record, in the Southeast, Royal Matron.

R. M.—Honored Secretary, what are your duties?

SEC.—To observe the proceedings of the Court and make proper record thereof, to receive all monies belonging to the Court and pay the same to the Treasurer, taking a receipt therefor, and perform the constitutional duties of my office.

R. M.—Where is the Sir Knight Associate Patron stationed?

SEC.—In the West, at the left of the Honored Associate Matron.

R. M.—Sir Knight Associate Patron, what are your duties?

A. P.—To preside in the absence of the Royal Patron and assist in the discharge of his duties.

R. M.—Where is the Honored Associate Matron stationed?

A. P. *or* SEC.—In the West, Royal Matron.

R. M.—Honored Associate Matron, what are your duties.

A. M.—To assist the Royal Matron in the discharge of her duties, and in her absence to preside and perform the executive duties of her office.

R. M.—Where is the Royal Patron stationed?

A. M.—On the throne, in the East, Royal Matron.

R. M.—Royal Patron, what are your duties?

R. P.—To see that none of the requirements of the Court are omitted or slighted; to preside at the advancement of candidates, and to perform all other duties required by this Court and the Constitution and Regulations of the Supreme Council and Grand Court.

R. M.—Honored Associate Matron, where is the Royal Matron stationed?

A. M.—On the throne, at the right of the Royal Patron, Royal Matron.

R. M.—What are her duties?

A. M.—To preside at the business meetings of the Court; to assist at the advancement of candidates, and to perform such other duties as may be required by the By-laws of the Court and the Constitution of the Supreme Council and Grand Court.

R. M.—(*Court is called up* ***) Honored Associate Conductress, attend at the Altar, and display the Holy Scriptures, with the appropriate emblem.

(*A. C. opens the Bible, on which she places the Amaranthine Wreath, salutes the R. M., and resumes her place.*)

R. M.—Royal Patron[1] perform the services appropriate to the occasion.

---

[1] Or *Chaplain, if this office is used.*

(R. P. goes to the Altar, west side, facing the East, and repeats the following, or other appropriate prayer):

R. P.—Almighty and merciful God, give unto us a more thorough understanding of Truth, Faith, Wisdom, and Charity. Pour down upon us an abundance of Thy grace, and give us such a sense of Thy loving-kindness that our hearts may be enabled to show forth Thy praise with our lips and in our lives, so that at last we may come into the eternal joy promised by Him Who hath taught us, when we pray, to say: *(All repeat aloud the Lord's Prayer.)*

(R. P. returns to his station.)

R. M.—Honored Ladies and Sir Knights, join in singing our opening ode.

ODE

R. M.—* *(seats the Court)*

R. M.—Honored Herald, make proclamation that the ceremony of opening .... Court No. .... on the Royal and Exalted degree of the Amaranth is complete, and command that the utmost courtesy and decorum be observed by all present.

HERALD—*(steps to the altar with the standard)* By order of the Royal Matron, I declare the ceremony of opening .... Court No. .... on the Royal and Exalted degree of the Amaranth complete. Honored Ladies and Sir Knights, let the utmost courtesy and decorum be observed by all present.

(*Places the Standard in the East and resumes her station.*)

R. M.—And now, with absolute nobleness of purpose, let us place confidence in each other. Let the strictest courtesy be observed, joined with the most refined and delicate attention. Let all things said or done be so charged with unselfishness and guided by Truth, Faith, Wisdom and Charity that, when we depart hence, we may rejoice to say, it was good for us to have been here. Honored Warder, inform the Sentinel that the Court is now open.

WAR.—Sir Knight Sentinel, this Court is now open.

WAR.—The Sentinel is informed, Royal Matron.

(*The Court is called to order, and proceeds with the regular business.*)

ORDER OF BUSINESS

1. Opening.
2. Roll call of officers.
3. Reading minutes of previous meeting.
4. Sickness and distress.
5. Petitions for membership.
6. Reports on petitions.
7. Balloting for candidates.
8. Conferring the degree.
9. Reports of committees.
10. Reading of communications.
11. Unfinished business.
12. New business.
13. Reading and approving bills.
14. Reading and approving minutes.
15. Closing.

CLOSING CEREMONY

R. M.—Royal Patron, have you any further business to offer before the Court is closed?

R. P.—*Answers.*

R. M.—Honored Associate Matron, have you any business to offer before we close?

A. M.—*Answers.*

R. M.—Has any Honored Lady or Sir Knight anything to offer before we close? *(Response or no response.)* Honored Secretary, read the minutes of this communication.

(The minutes are read and approved.)

R. M.—Honored Herald, proclaim to the Honored Ladies and Sir Knights that I am about to close this Court.

(Herald marches to the East, making square corners, takes the Standard and marches to a position between the East and Altar. Rests the Standard on the floor and remains in this position until the Court is closed.)

HER.—Honored Ladies and Sir Knights, by order of the Royal Matron, I proclaim to you and each of you that this Court is about to be closed.

R. M.—Honored Warder, make known to the Sentinel our commands, and bid him see that no interruption from without shall mar the solemnity of our closing ceremonies. *(The order is obeyed.)*

WAR.—Royal Matron, the Sentinel has your commands, and they will be obeyed.

Note.—*When pressed for time, this ceremony may be shortened by omitting all that is enclosed within brackets [ ].*

[R. M.—Honored Ladies and Sir Knights, it is proper that this Court be now closed. Honor us with your courteous attention, for the formula we present expresses some of the purest sentiments of our Order. In the prosaic affairs of human life the culture of noble and advanced thoughts must often be suspended for the exercise of sterner duties. Such is the case at present. This assembly, however delightful to mind and heart, however instructive as a school of courteousness and decorum, must be terminated. We must part, and this chain of sacred friendship must, for the time, be broken. It is, therefore, our request that a brief interchange of the courtesies of the Order be observed. By these we shall soften toil, lessen the hardships of life, and secure hopes of reunion. Royal Patron, you will lead in our parting ceremony.

Two blows of the gavel (**) call up the officers, who remain standing until the Court is closed.

[R. P.—Honored Ladies and Sir Knights, in the light of the King's countenance there is life; and his favor is as a bright bow after the latter rain. May the dews of heaven fall lightly upon us, until we meet again.

[A. M.—Those who have friends must show

themselves friendly. May the spirit of pure friendship guard us on the right hand and on the left, until we meet again.

[A. P.—*May we be guided only by the highest, noblest and purest things in life, until we meet again.*

[COND.—May the kingdom of God, which is righteousness, and joy, and peace, rest and abide with us, until we meet again.

[A. C.—Being rich in good works, unto the pure all things are pure. Whatsoever things are honest, just, and of good report let us accept and promote, until we meet again.

[TREAS.—He that gains wisdom, loveth his own soul. He that keepeth understanding, shall find good. May the All-Wise inspire us to secure that wisdom that is from above, that is full of mercy and good fruits, until we meet again.

[SEC.—He that is slow to anger is better than the mighty. And he that ruleth his spirit is greater than he that taketh a city. May we have command of the tongue, and never inscribe words except such as tend to peace, until we meet again.

[R. M.—What are the chief duties of members of the Royal and Exalted degree of the Amaranth?

[TRUTH—To speak the words of truth. The language of truth is pure and simple. Those who have truth in their hearts will not veil or lessen her beauty by deceitful decorations.

[FAITH—To cultivate abiding faith, for faith is the golden chain that binds humanity to Divinity.

[WISDOM—To acquire the wealth of wisdom. Wisdom's ways are ways of pleasantness, and all her paths are peace. It is our best interest to pursue the path of wisdom, having no regard to the obstacles which may lie in our course.

[CHARITY—To overlook the errors and faults of others, and practice acts of charity, the crowning glory of our Order.

[HER.—To carry glad tidings to the afflicted. If an enemy hunger, feed him; if he thirst, give him drink.

[M. in E.—May we be true to one another and loyal to the Flag of our Country.

[M. in W.—May we be faithful in the performance of every duty, for a good name is better than riches.

[CHAP.—*As the history of our lives is written daily, so may each moment be filled with thoughts of kindness and fraternal love.*

[WAR.—To carefully guard every avenue to the heart, and in the performance of the divine precepts expressed, let us continue vigilant and steadfast, until we meet again!]

———

R. M.—*** (*Court is called up*) Honored Ladies and Sir Knights, unite in singing our closing ode.

DOXOLOGY

Praise God from Whom all blessings flow;
Praise Him all creatures here below;
Praise Him above ye heavenly host;
Praise Father, Son and Holy Ghost.
(*Or some appropriate ode*)
(*R. P., raising his hands, will repeat the following, or other appropriate benediction.*)

R. P.—The Lord bless and keep you. The Lord lift up the light of His countenance upon you, and give you peace, now and evermore.

ALL RESPOND—Amen.

R. M.—Honored Associate Conductress, attend at the Altar and close the Sacred Volume.

(*A. C. approaches the Altar slowly and closes Bible, then returns to her station.*)

R. M.—Honored Ladies and Sir Knights, this Court is closed until our next regular meeting, unless sooner convened, in which event every member will have due and timely notice. Go in peace, and may all the recollections of this meeting be fragrant in our memories until time shall be no more.

(*R. M. gives the sign of the degree, and all the members respond: "Sweet in memory."*)

R. M.—I now declare .... Court No. ....
closed.

R. M.—Honored Warder, inform the Sentinel that the Court is closed and see that the portals of the Court room are opened.

WAR.—Sir Knight Sentinel, this Court is now closed.

R. M.—Honored Ladies and Sir Knights, Farewell. (*)

ALL—Farewell.

PRELIMINARY PREPARATIONS AND INSTRUCTIONS FOR CONFERRING THE DEGREE

The following properties should be at the proper places before the candidates are brought in so that there may be no confusion or waiting:

CHAIRS in the Northeast for the candidates and Conductresses. If folding chairs are used, they should be opened before the initiation starts to avoid unnecessary noise during the solemnity of the work.

SWORD for the accolade is at the station of the Royal Patron.

FONT with a small TOWEL for each candidate.

Two small PATENS, or dishes, with small pieces of BREAD and SALT on a silver tray, and all covered with a white NAPKIN should be placed on the pedestal of the A. C. where she can get them quickly and carry same to the Altar when instructed to do so.

If desired, two WREATHS may be used, one remaining on the Bible and the other on the Associate Matron's pedestal.

If there is more than one candidate, the Associate Conductress will escort the last one in line. offering her left arm to the candidate. The Conductress offers her right arm to the candidate she escorts.

In marching, always keep about three paces apart and turn square corners.

The Standard should be carried with the right hand close to the body, leaving the left hand free to hold the lower corner of the Standard and so keep it from swinging during the marching.

CONFERRING THE DEGREE

R. M.—Honored Associate Conductress, retire and ascertain if there are candidates in waiting to receive the degree of the Amaranth, and report to the Royal Patron.

(*She hands the gavel to the R. P. and he now takes charge.*)

(*A. C. retires, and finding a candidate in waiting, obtains her name and ascertains that she has received the Eastern Star degree; A. C. returns to the Court room and reports*):

A. C.—Royal Patron, there is in waiting Sister[1] .... (*giving name*)—who has received the degree of the Eastern Star, and now desires to be advanced to the Royal and Exalted degree of the Amaranth.

R. P.—Honored Secretary, has this candidate been elected to receive the degree of the Amaranth?

SEC.—She has, Royal Patron.

R. P.—Honored Ladies and Sir Knights, I am informed that sister .... (*giving name*)— having received the Eastern Star degree, is in waiting to receive the Royal and Exalted degree of the Amaranth. It, therefore, becomes my duty to as-

---

[1] *In case of several candidates, they will be named in order, and so introduced. Also, all questions and answers must be varied to correspond. If the candidate is a Master Mason, the wording should be changed accordingly.*

sist in conferring this degree upon her. Honored Associate Conductress and Honored Herald, retire to the anteroom, where you will find sister .... (*naming*)—to whom you will propound the usual questions required by the rules of the Order, and, if satisfactorily answered, prepare her for the ceremonies of this degree, and, when so prepared, apply for admission in due form.

MUSIC

(*Associate Conductress and Herald, taking Standard from the East, retire to the anteroom, where the A. C. will address the candidate*):

A. C.—Sister ...., before conducting you into the Court for advancement into our Rite, I am directed to propound to you certain questions, to which I expect decided and satisfactory answers. Do you present yourself here of your own free will?

CAND.—I do.

A. C.—Have you carefully considered the step you are about to take?

CAND.—I have.

A. C.—Know, then, that none can be advanced to the degree of the Amaranth except those who are earnest and sincere, whose benevolence is well assured, and whose zeal is untiring. Upon these conditions, do you desire to unite with us in our good work?

CAND.—I do.

(*The questions having been answered in the affirmative, the candidate is prepared by the removal of her hat, gloves, and coat, and led by the A. C. to the inner door of the Court room. Herald gives * * * raps on the door, when the Conductress will announce*):

COND.—Honored Associate Matron, there is an alarm at the inner door of the Court.

A. M.—Royal Patron, there is an alarm at the inner door of the Court.

R. P.—Honored Associate Matron, ascertain the cause of the alarm.

A. M.—Honored Conductress, ascertain the cause of the alarm.

(*Cond. proceeds to the door, gives * * * raps, opens the door, and asks*):

COND.—Why this alarm?

A. C.—The Associate Conductress and Herald have in charge a candidate for the honors of the Royal and Exalted degree of the Amaranth.

COND.—Does she desire to continue to unite with us in our good work?

A. C.—She does.

COND.—Has she carefully considered the step she is about to take?

A. C.—She has so answered.

COND.—Has she been informed that none ought to enter here, except the earnest and sincere, whose benevolence is well assured and whose zeal is untiring?

A. C.—She has.

COND.—Who vouches for her?

A. C.—We vouch for her.

COND.—Wait until your request is made known and the answer returned. (*closes the door*) Honored Associate Matron, the alarm was made by the Honored Associate Conductress and Honored Herald, having in charge a candidate for the honors of the Royal and Exalted degree of the Amaranth.

A. M.—Has she carefully considered the step she is about to take?

COND.—She has.

A. M.—Does she desire to continue to unite with us in our good work?

COND.—She does.

A. M.—Who vouches for her?

COND.—Our Honored Associate Conductress and Honored Herald.

A. M.—Royal Patron, the alarm was made by the Honored Associate Conductress and Honored Herald, having in charge a candidate for the honors of the Royal and Exalted degree of the Amaranth.

R. P.—Have all the necessary questions been asked in regard to her qualifications, and her desire to unite with us in our good work?

A. M.—They have, and her answers are satisfactory.

R. P.—Who vouches for her?

A. M.—Our Honored Associate Conductress and Honored Herald.

R. P.—Admit them.

A. M.—Honored Conductress, admit our Honored Associate Conductress and Honored Herald, together with the sister who comes so warmly recommended.

COND.—(*opens the door and addresses the candidate*): Your answers to the questions are satisfactory and evince the purity of your intentions; therefore, our Royal Patron orders that you be admitted. Be assured that a cordial welcome awaits you.

R. P.—*** (*Court is called up*)

MUSIC

(*Herald enters, leading the line of march, takes the Standard in her right hand, leads to the Font, forming a circle; candidates between Conductresses.*

As they enter the Court room, following the Herald, the Conductress offers her right arm to the first candidate in line and the Associate Conductress offers her left arm to the last candidate in the line If there are more than two candidates, they marcn in twos and are instructed to take each other's arm.

As soon as the line of march has entered, the door is closed.

(*When the music or song is finished, Cond. says*):

COND.—In the Ancient Mysteries, preparatory to initiation, the candidate was required to perform the Ceremony of Ablution,[1] by washing of hands in pure water, as a symbol of the purification of the heart, and as a solemn pledge of future decorum and rectitude. If you are willing to give us the same pledge, do so by the same symbol.

(*Cond. pauses while all candidates step forward to the Font in a body, if possible. While candidates are performing this ceremony, Cond. says*):

COND.—I will wash my hands in innocency, and thus shall I accomplish Thy Courts, Oh, Lord.

(*The Conductresses now offer the towels to the candidates. If the class is too large to assemble around the Font at the same time, the Conductresses will divide them in groups and the Cond. will deliver her charge to each group as they perform the ceremony.*)

(*The line forms into marching formation, led by the Herald, followed by Cond. and first candidate in*)

---

[1] *The use of water as a symbol of purification and consecration to duty has descended to us from the remotest ages, and was of universal practice among the nations of antiquity, and is not, therefore, the exclusive property of any religion. In using it we do not pretend to imitate or interfere with any rite or any organization. The ceremonial we perform is not of a showy character, by which the Order seeks to intrude itself upon the world. It teaches neither hatred, intolerance, nor revenge. In this ceremony the Lustration is a symbol of the purity of the soul and correctness of life. It also teaches those primary truths on which all religions must repose; and inculcates those principles of pure morality which have commended themselves to the good and wise of all ages.*

DIAGRAM 3

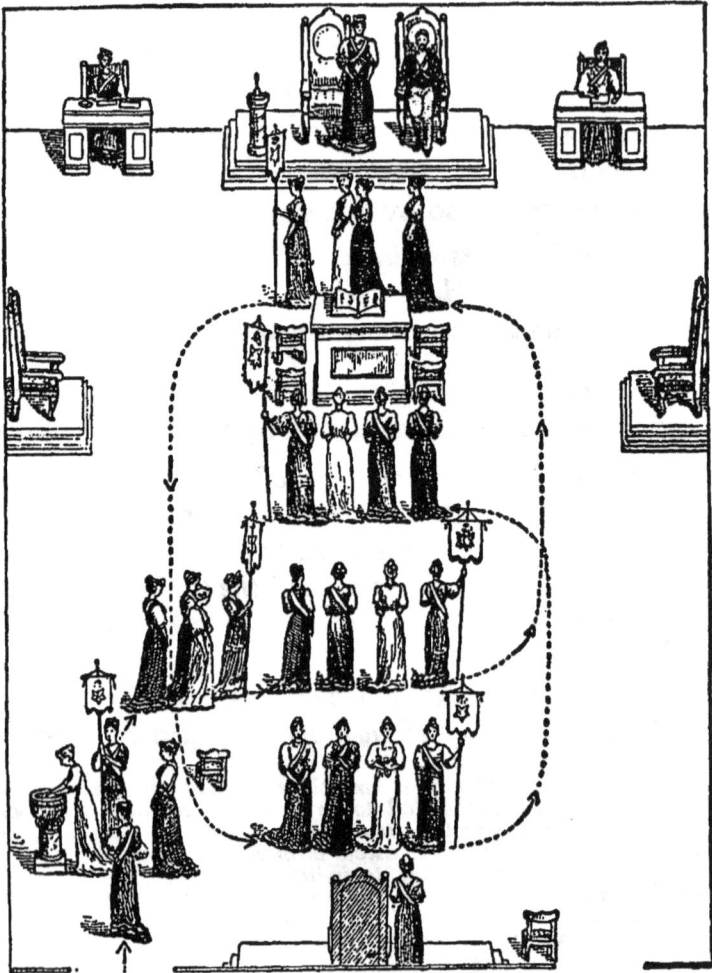

line, etc. to center of room between Altar and A.M.'s station, facing East. See Diagram 3. The following, or other appropriate music):

TUNE—*Downs.* C. M.

Come, spirit of celestial love,
  With might and pow'r divine,
Upon Thy servant from above
  Let heavenly graces shine.

R. P.—* (*Court is seated*)   Let the candidate journey from the West by way of the South to the East, and by the North to the West again, and thence to the Altar.

(*The procession proceeds, Herald leading, followed by Cond. and cand., and A. C.*)

SOFT MUSIC

COND.—(*as they journey*)   May thy pathways be strewn with flowers.   That which you find to do strive to do with your best ability, abandoning all anxiety for the results.   The fruit of your toil is ever before you; reach out your hand and gather it.

(*The procession will halt before the throne without changing position, when the R. M. will say*):

R. M.—Our good deeds and kindly offices performed for others are the angels that watch over and smile upon us in our dreams.   To thy faith add knowledge, to thy actions, love, and thy presence among people will be a benediction. Make good use of time if you value eternity. Yesterday cannot be recalled; tomorrow cannot be assured; today only is yours, which, if you procrastinate, you lose —which loss is forever. The common mind usually condemns those who have the courage to enter the field of progress.

(*They proceed by way of the North to the West.*)

COND.—(*as they proceed*) Those who look only for the evil will find the evil; but the life of those who look only for the good and the pure, the unselfish and noble—the truth of all things—becomes a living fountain of wisdom and understanding.

(*Halt before A. M., who will say*):

A. M.—The light of the body is the eye. If, therefore, thine eye be just, thy whole body shall be full of light; but if thine eye be evil, thy whole body shall be full of darkness. God gives to large and expansive minds broad and lofty views. Advanced thought and ideas are enlightening the world. Many great heralds of truths in the past have suffered a martyr's doom, to end in an overwhelming defeat to their enemies—*for God is just.*

COND.—(*as they turn and approach the Altar*) A cheerful smile and kind word linger long in memory, gilding with beauty the darkest hours of life.

(*The second verse is sung*):
> Remove afar all dread or fear,
> All doubt and burdened care;
> Protect her as she enters here
> In all our work to share.

COND.—Royal Patron, it is my privilege to introduce to you Sister .... (*giving name*), who has been initiated in the degree of the Eastern Star, and her desire is to be advanced into the Royal and Exalted degree of the Amaranth, and be acknowledged a member of this Court.

R. P.—Sister ...., as a welcome guest, you stand before our Altar. You see spread open thereon the inspired Word of God, the fountain of grace, and love, and truth, and the Amaranthine wreath appropriately rests thereon. Your desire is to participate in the privileges of the Royal and Exalted degree of the Amaranth. What motives induced you to seek admission into this Order?

CAND. (*prompted by Cond.*)—The desire to acquire knowledge and make progress in the ways of wisdom, benevolence, and virtue.

R. P.—Do you feel that you are endowed with sufficient fortitude to meet difficulties and enlarge your sphere of usefulness, by means of your virtues and our example, your labors with our assistance?

CAND.—I do.

R. P.—Will you be able to endure the sarcasms of the ignorant, who will be the more inclined to make you their victim because the principles we inculcate are unknown to them?

CAND. (*prompted by Cond.*)—I believe I will be able to do so.

R. P.—What do you deem to be your duty to your neighbor?

CAND. (*prompted by Cond.*)—To do unto others as I would that they should do unto me.

TABLEAU AT ALTAR

DIAGRAM 4

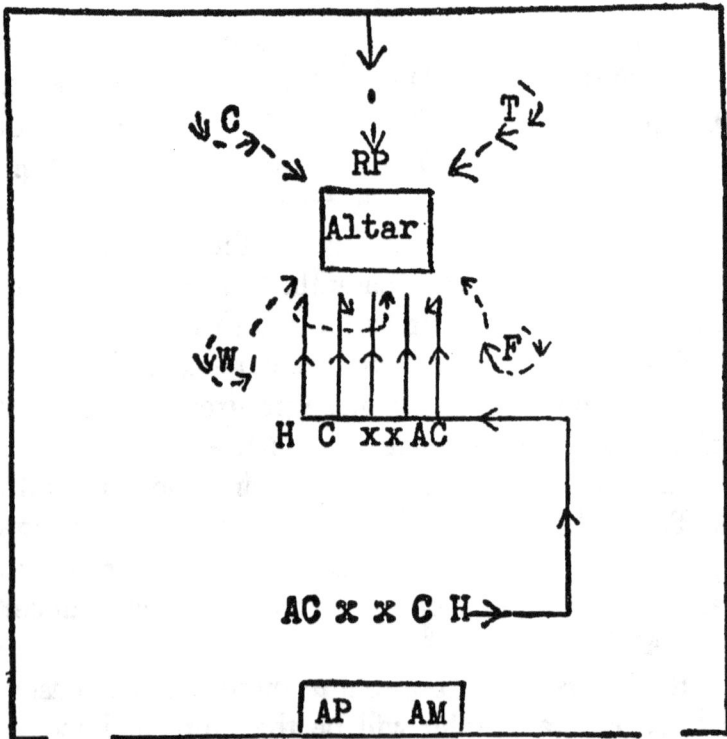

R. P.—You have answered our questions in a manner that assures us of your sincerity and inspires us with confidence in your fidelity and courage. It is therefore eminently proper that we should receive you among us. We cannot enlist too many such laborers in our good work. Having been vouched for in terms which the usages of the Order require is proof to us that you will render valuable aid to our cause. Being satisfied with your qualifications and earnestness, the Court is united in granting your request. With this knowledge of our noble purposes are you willing to assume the obligations and responsibilities that may be required of you by the rules of the Order?

CAND.—I am.

R. P.—Honored Conductress and Honored Associate Conductress, ** (1) **

R. P.—*** (*Court is called up*)

(*Cand.* ** (2) ** *Cond. on the left and A. C. on the right, one step in the rear; Herald, with standard, in the center; Truth, Faith, Wisdom, and Charity, right and left; all forming a tableau. R. P. steps to the altar, and says*):

R. P.—That you may truly represent the Order, maintain its honor, and faithfully preserve ** (3) ** These are the covenant vows of the Royal and Exalted degree of the Amaranth, which we are all under obligation to keep.

*(R. P. returns to the throne, * Court is seated. Group remain at the altar.)*

R. P.—Honored Associate Conductress, present the sacred emblems.

SOFT MUSIC

(A. C. brings forward the emblems—the patens containing bread and salt on a salver, covered with a

*white napkin—and places them on the altar, Cond. at
the left and A. C. at the right of the candidate, and
other officers in semicircle, as before. R. M. descends
from the throne to the altar.*)

R. M.—The ceremony in which we now ask you
to engage is to partake with us of the sacred emblems of Friendship and Hospitality—bread and
salt. (*A. C. uncovers patens of bread and salt.*)
Bread is for nourishment, and salt for preservation.
When the Master formed the prayer, the model of
supplication for all ages, He taught us to say:
"Give us this day our daily bread." This ceremony
was practiced by the Ancients, and is used to this
day among many peoples. You will easily compre-
hend its significance. To share bread and salt with
another is to exchange confidence and pledge hospitality. In thus partaking with you of these emblems, it is with the wish that you may be nour-
ished by the true Bread of life, and that your days
may be prolonged and made happy, even as you
shall strive to nourish others, and practice the noblest deeds of charity, in your daily intercourse
with the world. If you can, in truth and sincerity
of purpose, fulfill these sacred requirements, partake
with us of these emblems, and we will in the same
spirit share them with you.

(*R. M. and cand., Cond., and A. C. partake of the
bread and taste the salt.*)

R. M.—By this act we, in behalf of this Court, seal and make perpetual our mutual bond of friendship.

(*A. C. removes the patens. R. P. descends and conducts the R. M. to the throne.*)

R. P.—* (*Court is seated*)

(*Cond. escorts cand. to the northeast part of the room, and all are seated.*)

R. M.—Honored Ladies, who form the square near the Altar, respectively, and in due order, explain to the candidate the beauties and usefulness of this degree, and the practical lessons which it inculcates.

(*Officers rise, successively, step to the corner of the Altar, near their stations, and repeat the following*):

TRUTH—The Royal and Exalted degree of the Amaranth is practical in all its parts, teaching benevolence, honor, the purest morality, and the strictest adherence to TRUTH. As you advance in this degree you will find at every turn new incentives to goodness. The allegories and traditions embodied in its lectures are full of instruction. The broad streams of knowledge that are open to all inquirers in the present age must be traced to their sources if you would acquire the genuine meaning of their symbols and the mystic forms that make up this system.

From the earliest records of time, and following the course of history, we find everywhere the elements of Truth—the universal principles of human thought and action. Generation after generation passes away, but Truth remains forever the same. It is the life-blood of human power, the intellectual air we breathe. Without this attribute society could not subsist for a single hour; governments, laws, institutions, religion, the manners and customs of humanity, all bear the indelible imprint of its universality and indestructibility. Then let Truth be the beacon-light upon which your eye is fixed. It will surely guide you over the stormiest seas. There is wondrous vitality in error, and against it we must ever be on our guard. Truth may conquer slowly; violence and falsehood may impair it for a time, but its future cannot be destroyed.

"The eternal years of God are hers."

This degree, as before said, is practical. It calls the attention of the wise to subjects rare and elevating. It instructs the illiterate, extends consolation to the unhappy, material aid to the needy, and, finally, it offers bonds of friendship interwoven with the purest principles of Truth and Morality.

MUSIC

(*Truth resumes her seat. Faith steps forward, and says*):

FAITH—In the daily affairs of life you should have a constant FAITH. A faith in God, Who rules in all things; a faith in your own ability, which insures success. Our faith is all our own, held direct from God. Through all the changes of an uncertain world our faith in an overruling Providence must never be shaken. It must be strong and permanent. A confidence in the assistance and protection of an Almighty Being naturally produces patience, hope, cheerfulness, and all other happy dispositions of the mind that alleviate those calamities which we are not otherwise able to remove.

In times of adversity, amid the scenes of poverty and affliction, and even in the gloomy hour of death, the possession of this virtue brings comfort and hopeful resignation. A breach of faith is a crime that brings a stain on a nation, for faith ought to be kept even with an enemy.

The age of chivalry was the age of undeviating faith and unblemished honor. It was the period when the *word* was as strong a bond as the *oath*. Among the sublime principles of chivalry it held in faithful reverence the protection of woman. To us has been handed down this sacred trust in its purity, and it becomes our highest honor to maintain and perpetuate it.

We claim honor and integrity as essential qualities in the Ladies and Knights of the Amaranth. While you possess them you will be worthy of the title—a peerless dignity—the most distinguished in our power to bestow.

MUSIC

(Faith resumes her seat. Wisdom steps forward and says):

WISDOM—WISDOM embraces the whole of practical knowledge. It is that perfection of an intelligent agent by which he is enabled to select and employ the most useful means in order to accomplish proper and substantial results. An ancient lawgiver, being asked if his code of laws was the best that could be given his countrymen, replied: "It is the best they are capable of receiving"—a profound utterance, easily comprehended and applicable to human life in our day.

"There was a little city," says the Preacher, "and few men within it; and there came a great king against it and besieged it, and built great bulwarks about it. Now, there was found in it a poor wise man, and he, by his wisdom, delivered the city; yet no man remembered that same poor man. Then, said I, 'Wisdom is better than strength'; nevertheless, the poor man's wisdom is despised, and his words are not heard."

Should your efforts of usefulness be met by indifference and ingratitude, be not discouraged thereby. The code of regulations of this degree makes the moral obligation absolute; and, therefore, the practice of the moral virtues essential. We would unite to elevate and purify the standard of good in an evil world. This we propose to do by putting pure and noble ideas into practice, and inculcating the best precepts at our command. We are advocates of the nobility of labor. Rank and title, however honorable, are not incompatible with efficient work with hand and brain. Many great deeds have their inception in the small struggles of life. There are noble and mysterious triumphs which no human eye beholds, which no renown rewards, which no flourish of trumpets heralds.

He most lives,
Who thinks most, feels the noblest, acts the best.

MUSIC

(*Wisdom resumes her seat. Charity steps forward, and says*):

CHARITY—CHARITY stands as the pearl of great price among the virtues—"for the greatest of these is Charity." It beautifies all our actions and enlarges the desires of the heart to do good. That Charity is enduring which flows from an innate sense of duty. That Charity is truest and noblest which treads in secret the paths of poverty, unseen and unproclaimed; but, like the great laws of nature, does the work of God in silence, looking only to a better world for its reward. It is the attribute of divine love, and the most universal religion of mankind. There is no law that circumscribes the compensation that may result from a single good deed. The smallest actual good performed is better than the most magnificent promise.

The benefits produced by our labor relate to the present and the future. There is a beautiful thought conveyed in a legend, that on the shores of the Adriatic Sea the wives of the fishermen, whose husbands have gone far off upon the deep, are in the habit, at even-tide, of going down to the sea-shore and singing the first verse of a favorite hymn.[1] After they have sung it, they listen till they hear,

---

[1] *When possible to do so, a choir of ladies and gentlemen will sing two verses of a familiar hymn; the ladies, being in the eastern part of the Court room, will sing the first verse.*

borne by the wind across the desert sea, the second verse,[1] sung by their husbands as they are tossed by the gale upon the waves, thus rendering happiness to all.

Perhaps, if we listen, we, too, may hear, in this desert world, some whisper borne from afar, to remind us that there is a heavenly home; and when we sing a hymn upon earth, it may be we shall hear its echo breaking in sweet melody upon the sands of time, cheering the hearts of those who, perchance, are pilgrims and strangers, looking for a city that hath sure foundations.

Honored Ladies and Sir Knights of the Royal and Exalted degree of the Amaranth will deserve this title if they have strength, faith, and energy to obtain a glorious victory in the achievement of good works.

MUSIC

(*Charity resumes her seat. Cond. and cand. rise, and Cond. says*):

COND.—Royal Matron, our sister has voluntarily accepted the covenant vows of the Amaranth, and now stands pledged before you.

R. M.—Honored Ladies and Sir Knights, the earnest and devout manner in which this sister has assumed the solemn vows of the degree assures me

---

[1] *The gentlemen, in an adjoining room, with the door ajar, will sing the second verse, and all join in the chorus.*

that we may safely receive her into full membership with us. Therefore, in behalf of the members
of this Court, and of the Royal and Exalted degree
of the Amaranth, I will proceed to confer its honors upon her. Honored Conductress, accompany
our sister to the proper place for that purpose.

SOFT MUSIC

*(The candidate is conducted via the North to the
west side of the Altar, facing the East.)*

R. M.—Honored Conductress, the West is the
place of the setting sun, the verge of the twilight
gloom, and darkness of the night. In its uncertain
light, amid the shadows of the declining day, the
beauties of our work cannot be revealed. It is the
rising, not the setting, sun that we adore. I pray
you do not tarry there.

MUSIC

*(Cand. is conducted via the South to the East, in
front of the throne.)*

R. M.—The East is that quarter from which the
bright morning star heralds the approach of day,
and the proper place for honorable advancement.
Before the rising sun, darkness disappears, and
light covers the surface of the earth. Here, the
light, arising from the blessings of our Order as the
radiance from the morning sun, awaits the neo-

phyte. Place our sister in the proper position, to receive the dignified honor of the accolade.

MUSIC

(Cand. is caused to kneel on a cushion at the foot of the throne.)

R. P.—°°° *(Court is called up)*

(A. C., Faith, and Charity on the North side; Truth, Wisdom, and Warder, on the South side, form a semicircle behind the candidate. Herald, with Standard, forms the center of the tableau.)

(R. M. wears a crown and represents a queen. R. P. hands a sword to R. M.)

R. M.—The ceremony by which Knighthood is conferred is called the accolade. Conforming to this custom, and by the authority vested in me, I receive you *(places the sword on the left and right shoulders, and on the head of the candidate)*, and confer upon you the dignity of a Lady of the Royal and Exalted degree of the Amaranth *(carries sword)*; and as the Amaranthine flower is typical of undying friendship and eternal truth, so with this right hand accept our pledge of an abiding trust, and a cordial reception into our fellowship.[1] *(Assists her to rise.)*

The sword is a weapon of warfare. It teaches us to be always watchful in the battle of life, and with the Sword of the Spirit, which is the Word of God, to guard every approach to the heart, that the evil tendencies of our nature may not overcome the good. Let us strike valiantly against vice that degrades; against ignorance that blinds, against prejudice that warps our judgment, and against hatred and malice that bring only discontent and misery.

---

[1] *During this ceremony, the R. M. should not leave the throne. If other candidates, the ceremony must be repeated.*

Keep this lesson ever before you, and by the symbolic use of this glittering blade cover your name

with honor, and become a blessing to those with whom you are associated.[1]   Conduct the candidate

---

[1] *If the candidate is a Master Mason, he is not crowned with the Amaranthine wreath, but is conducted to west of the*

to our Honored Associate Matron, for additional honors.

MUSIC

(*Cond. escorts cand. to the West, followed by A. C., Herald, with standard; Truth, Faith, Wisdom, Charity and Warder. Cond., in passing, takes the wreath from the Altar to the A. M., unless two wreaths are used and one is already on the A. M.'s pedestal.*)

COND.—Honored Associate Matron, by order of the Royal Matron, I present our sister to you for additional honors.

A. M.—The order of our Royal Matron shall be obeyed (*holding up the wreath*). The Amaranthine wreath is the peculiar emblem of the Order. Because of the lasting nature of its bloom, the Amaranth was regarded by many of the ancients as the symbol of immortality. The possession of its early blossoms inspired the belief that the soul would enjoy eternal rest in the realms of the Celestial Home. And now, as an additional memento to confirm our friendship, we crown (*placing the wreath on the head of the candidate*) you with the emblem of the Crown of Life.

Altar and addressed by the R. M. as "My brother, in addition to your obligation of secrecy, you are required to protect and defend the Standard of the Order," etc. See page 100 and continue ceremony to the end.

If desired, the lecture by the Royal Patron beginning on page 106 may be substituted for the R. M.'s address, page 103.

This is no diadem of gold; no cincture of pearls; no regal tiara; no frame-work of gems, velvet-lined, like that which so often presses upon the aching brows of royalty. That is a badge of power, frequently empty, unsubstantial, and delusive. But our crown and our act of coronation have a higher and a nobler meaning. We crown you as being eminent for virtue, zeal, and well-doing, showing charity to the destitute, and faithful in every walk of life.

May all your footsteps fall upon flowers. May all your good intentions be fraught with success. May your last days be your best. We crown you in the hope of immortality. There is no death to the pure and loving. May your admission to the land Celestial and Everlasting be sure, and your entrance full of delight. And as the years roll along and bring about the great consummation for which we all hopefully wait, may your ransomed spirit be crowned with the never-ceasing favor of Almighty God.

(*The following, or any appropriate hymn, is sung by the Court.*)

TUNE—*Coronation.* C. M.

Oh, crown immortal, wreath sublime,
 That speaks the joys unseen;
Its leaves defy the frosts of time;
 'Tis heaven's unfading green.

NOTE.—*If there be other candidates, the same cere-mony of coronation will be performed on each.*

MUSIC

R. P.—° (*Court is seated*)

(*Officers, except Cond. and Herald, with Standard,
return to their stations. Cond. returns the wreath to*

the Bible unless two are used, and escorts cand. to west of Altar, facing the East, when the R. M. will say):

R. M.—My sister, in addition to your obligation of secrecy, you are required to protect and defend the Standard of the Order. Honored Herald, place the Standard in charge of our newly advanced sister.

(Herald hands the Standard to cand., who grasps the staff with the left hand, her right hand on her left breast; Cond. at her left and Herald at her right, two steps back. Herald goes to her station and gets the flag and returns to right of cand. R. P. steps from throne and says):

R. P.—My sister, it is the high privilege of my office to portray to you the significance of the Standard you now hold. It is the Grand Standard of our Rite of Adoption. Among the earliest assemblies of men for purposes of peace or war, some conspicuous emblem was adopted, expressive of the common sentiment, around which they might rally for mutual protection or special interest. The tribes of Israel had each its banner, corresponding with those used in the present day. Out of the ancient practice grew the custom, which is now universal, of using standards bearing emblematical figures, sacred or warlike, to distinguish private and national associations.

The Flag is the symbol of a Nation. To dishonor it is to insult the Nation. Beneath its folds the weakest are protected, while the strongest must submit to the authority of which it is an emblem. It canopies, with its protecting plications alike, the humblest hut and the loftiest mansion. In the distant regions of the globe the traveler, at the sight of his country's flag, is reminded of home and

(Herald solemnly waves flag over head of cand. until end of R. P.'s speech. Then returns flag to holder at her station.)

its endearing associations. The excitement of that moment, crowded with its heartfelt emotions, can never be forgotten.

(The following is sung by the Chapter or a choir):

HOME, SWEET HOME

'Mid pleasures and palaces though we may roam,
Be it ever so humble, there's no place like home.
A charm from the skies seems to hallow us there,
Which, seek through the world, is ne'er met with elsewhere.

> Home! Home! Sweet, sweet home!
> There's no place like home!
> There's no place like home!

R. P.—Bear in mind, my sister, that the Standard of the Order is no holiday standard, gorgeously emblazoned for gayety or vanity. No! It is the synonym of the banner of Eternal Truth. The All-Seeing-Eye upon it, with the winged messenger bearing the emblem of peace, should encourage you to walk in the path of virtue. You are required to defend the Standard on every proper occasion, and to be always faithful to the sublime principles of the Order, which, being founded on Truth and Charity, will ultimately spread through every land and among every people.

(*R. P. returns to the East and ascends the throne. Herald takes the Standard from the candidate and leads the Cond. and candidate to seats in the Northeast, where they may be seated. Herald then replaces the Standard in the East and marches to her station by way of the South.*)

R. P.—* (4) *

R. P.—The R. M. will now address you (*hands the gavel to the R. M.*).

R. M.—My sister, you have been regularly inducted into the Royal and Exalted degree of the Amaranth. We have joined in a bond of mutual friendship; our mysterious accolade has fallen upon you, we trust never to be recalled; the hand of fraternal welcome has been enclasped in yours, accompanied by the heart's holiest greeting, and you have been crowned with the emblem of the Crown of Life.

These ceremonies being completed, it is now my pleasing duty, in behalf of this Court, to congratulate you upon your reception. Your worthiness has entitled you to our distinguished consideration, and gives us confidence that by your life you will prove deserving of the favor we have at this time bestowed. May that life be prolonged in honor and usefulness. May you long continue a member in active fellowship, ever a faithful defender of the principles it inculcates.

You will now be conducted to the Place of Records, where you will sign the By-laws of the Court, and become entitled to all the privileges of membership, after which you will be reconducted to your present position.

(The cand. is conducted to the station of the Secretary, where she will sign the roll of membership. Returning to the foot of the throne, the R. M. will say):

R. M.—My sister, in the name of .... Court, No. ...., we receive and welcome you as an active member. May your name, now placed in our Book of Records, ever remain there, with increasing brightness, until such time as it shall be entered for perpetual record in the Everlasting Book of Life.

R. M.—*** *(Court is called up; cand. is caused to face the West)*

R. M.—Honored Ladies and Sir Knights, no one has appeared before us with higher claims to hon-

orable recognition than the sister who now stands
before you. We will, therefore, welcome her as an
active member of this Court.

(*The following or other appropriate hymn may be
sung.*)

AMERICA

Thrice welcome to our band,
By all our precepts stand,
    Find here a home.
Be faithful, good, and true,
All Virtue's paths pursue,
Then we will stand by you
    Whate'er may come.

R. M.—Honored Associate Matron, call the
Court to recreation, to resume at the sound of the
gavel in the East.

A. M.—Honored Ladies and Sir Knights, by order of the Royal Matron, you will now be at recreation, to resume at the sound of the gavel in the
East. *

(*The entire company join in giving a hearty welcome to the candidate. After a brief period, the
R. M. will call the Court to order, and proceed with
business.*)

INITIATION OF A MASTER MASON

The same ceremony is used to confer the degree on a Master Mason, but proper changes should be made in addressing him, etc. He is not crowned with the Amaranthine wreath, but is conducted to west of the Altar at that part of the ceremony and addressed by the Royal Matron:

R. M.—My brother, in addition to your obligation of secrecy, you are required to protect and defend the Standard of the Order, etc.

See page 100 and continue ceremony to the end.

If desired, the following lecture by the Royal Patron may be substituted for the address by the Royal Matron on page 103.

———

MY BROTHER: I congratulate you on being found worthy to become a member of this honorable Order. I purpose, on this your entrance to our companionship and love, to offer you a few thoughts on the life of man—his power and possibilities.

What a wonderful problem is human life; how mysterious its origin; how simple, yet how complex the marvelous machinery by which it is kept in motion. Whence comes the mysterious spark that makes an immortal soul? and how vitally important to us is its end! We are the inhabitants of one of the smallest of all the planets, while around us on every side are myriads of worlds and suns and systems, in the contemplation of which the soul bursts forth with all its anthem of praise. How wonderful are thy works, O God! We are standing today upon the threshold of time; tomorrow, perhaps, we shall stand within the portals of eternity. The man of towering intellect and giant strength moves among us, exciting our awe and admiration. Gazing on this the most perfect and beautiful of all God's works:

"What a piece of work is a man!
How noble in reason, how infinite in faculty;
In form and moving how express and admirable;
In action how like an angel;
In comprehension how like a god."

And yet by what a weak and uncertain tenure does this image of God hold the solemn mystery of life.

It has been said "that life is what we make it." As an abstract theory, yes. As a concrete principle, no. We are not the masters of ourselves. Constitutional inheritance rules us as with a rod of iron. Our environments in early life hem us in with influences that we never overcome from the cradle to the grave.

At the entrance to the groves of the Academy in Athens, where Sophocles studied and Plato taught, was emblazoned in letters of gold these words, "Man, know thyself." Here was the beginning and the end of human wisdom. For the man knowing himself would not only find his relation to the world around him, but, reaching out toward the glittering stars, would learn his relationship to those shining worlds that float forever in the immensity of space, and, for aught we know, teeming with a purer spiritual life, where countless millions of white-winged angels sing hallelujah to the Lord forevermore.

If this be the true condition of the future, the all-important question to us is, How can we reach this glory? How are we to secure this immortal reward?

Is there a divine and spiritual essence that will survive eternally this house of clay—a something that men call soul, and that is as indestructible as God himself? A something which shall survive the wreck of matter, and which can never, never die?

In this dire extremity, when the lifeless body of his brother lay bleeding and mangled on the earth before him, in answer to the inquiry of the Lord, "Where is thy brother?" the first murderer replied, "Am I my brother's keeper?" And that inquiry and reply have echoed down through the ages ever since the twilight of time. Yes, my brother, you are your brother's keeper, and from that obligation no power on earth can absolve you. In all this universe there is no such thing as absolute independence. Every particle of which this great globe is composed is dependent for its existence on every other particle, and the difference between the mightiest king and the poorest beggar is only a span. The same earth receives them both. In a little while they return to the elements from which they sprang.

What, then, are the lessons we learn from this life experience? Chiefly, that we live not for ourselves alone. The man who thinks only for himself is the most contemptible of human beings. The world owes him nothing, living or dead.

"Whatsoever thy hand findeth to do, do it with all thy heart." Consider why the Creator has endowed you with reason, that glorious faculty denied to all other living things. Within the bosom of nature are wondrous secrets, all the heritage of man, but only to be obtained by ceaseless labor. Such is the Divine decree.

Look out at yonder brilliant flash of light that descends from the heavens to the earth. Listen to the mighty voice that heralds the passage of God's swift messenger of life and death. Swift as thought it flies; more terrible than an army with banners. That is the wondrous power that rules the earth today. Nowhere are the genius and inspiration of man more evident than in the development of this mysterious and terrible agent, which seems to be in more direct communion with God than all the other powers in nature beside. The unseen and sightless courier of the air has been harnessed by man and made his obedient slave. It furnishes him with light as brilliant as the sun. It carries his messages thousands of miles under the sea. It speaks in the ear of friendship hundreds of miles away. It comes to the bed of sickness with wondrous healing power. It is man's willing servant, carrying him wherever he will; and for the punishment of crime it becomes the swift messenger of death. Marvel of marvels, miracle of miracles, who can prophesy the limit of thy power? Man is God's interpreter of the secrets of nature intrusted to his care. Down deep in the earth, over which lie the deposits and debris of unnumbered centuries, he reaches the story of this world's history, thousands of years before man was created. His plummet sounds the vast ocean's depths, once thought fathomless, and drags its hidden secrets to the light of day. All nature in the heavens above and in the earth beneath is man's inheritance.

Behold the glory of the heavens in a starry night. Nowhere does man seem nearer to God, and nowhere in nature is man's power as visible as it is in his communion with the stars. In the stillness of night, while gazing on the heavens, we seem to hear more clearly the voice of God, and to feel more intensely his visible presence.

The object of the association of which you form a part at this time is to lead you up to a higher, a better, and a nobler life.   From this time forth, so long as you may be found worthy of our companionship and love, you live not for yourself alone. Wherever you may wander in aftertime, if your needs should demand it, should you meet a brother or sister of this degree, they will afford you willing aid.

Be faithful to your vows.   Place honor before life.   Lastly, trust in God and fear not; that in the end you will receive the reward due to truthfulness and fidelity.

(The cand. is then conducted to the station of the Secretary, where he will sign the roll of membership and return to the foot of the throne.   Continue on with the ceremony, see pages 103–105.)

INSTALLATION CEREMONY— SUBORDINATE COURT

The ceremonies of installation may be performed in public, if desired, in which event the Court will be declared open and in order by one blow of the gavel. * The private ceremony of opening the Court should be omitted.

A *new* Court must be constituted and dedicated before the installation of its officers.

The Installing Officer of a new Court must be the Grand Royal Patron, or an authorized Deputy.

The Installing Officer of a chartered Court must be a present or Past Royal Patron, or a present or Past Grand Officer, and he will be addressed accordingly.

Officers cannot legally be installed by proxy. Installation of a reëlected officer is unnecessary.

The newly-elected Royal Patron and Royal Matron should be in possession of the Administrative degree before installation.

A Lady Marshal and a Sir Knight (usually a Past Royal Matron and Patron) should be selected in advance. The official jewels should be collected and placed convenient for use. A list of the officers to be installed will be furnished by the Secretary. If the ceremony is performed in public, an address on the purposes of the degree may be delivered by the Grand Royal Patron, or a Sir Knight selected for the occasion. Music—vocal and instrumental

—may be introduced with good effect. All things being in order, the ceremonies will proceed as follows:

INST. OFFICER—Honored Sisters and Sir Knights, there is, perhaps, no more important event in the history of the Court than the selection and installation of its officers, to carry forward the work of the body. The vital interests of the Court are confided to those who are chosen to fill the various stations, and the welfare of the Court and the prosperity of the Rite may be affected, for good or evil, by their action; therefore, the greatest care should be exercised in the selection of the proper persons to be office bearers. You have made your selection, and that they will perform their duties, in promoting the interests of this Court and the advancement of the Rite, is our belief. Before investing them with official authority, let us seek wisdom from that source whence wisdom comes. * * *

The Installing Officer, or Chaplain, offers the following, or other appropriate

PRAYER

Our Father, Who art in heaven, from Whom cometh all wisdom, look upon and bless us in the duties we are about to perform. May these officers who are at this time to be invested with authority to govern in this Court be impressed with the importance of the trusts confided to them. Endue them with wisdom, that they may rightly discharge every duty; with love, that they may exemplify the beauty of concord in all their doings; with fidelity, that they may not fail in the performance of any obligation; with fortitude, that they may fearlessly face every obstacle and conquer every difficulty. And grant that peace and harmony may prevail. Direct us in the ways of truth and love, and may all be done in Thy holy name. Amen.

RESPONSE—Amen.

I. O.—* (*Court is seated*)

I. O.—Honored Marshal, place the officers to be installed west of the Altar, facing the East.

(*The officers are placed in a line, west of the Altar, facing the East, the Matron, Patron, and Associate Matron being in the center, two steps in advance. Lady Marshal will say*):

MAR.—Royal Patron, the officers of .... Court, No. ...., have been elected and appointed to conduct its ceremonies and business affairs for the ensuing year. They stand before you, ready to assume the obligation of office.

I. O.—Honored Sisters and Sir Knights, before investing you with the badges and titles appropriate to your various stations, it becomes my duty to administer to you an obligation of faithfulness. Will you accept it in the kindly spirit it is offered, and comply with its demands in truth and obedience?

EACH OFFICER—I will.

I. O.—*** (*Court is called up*)

I. O.—Place your right hand on your left breast, and raise your left hand, and repeat after me:

I—(*pronounce your name*)—do solemnly promise, in the presence of the Supreme Ruler of the Universe and these witnesses, that I will, to the best of my ability, faithfully perform the duties of the office to which I have been elected. That I will support and maintain the Constitution of the Supreme Council, the Statutes and Regulations of the Grand Court of the State of ...., and the By-laws of this Court, and do all in my power to promote the prosperity of the Order.

I. O.—*

(*The officers may be seated on one side of the room. The Marshal will present the officers in order, beginning with the*

ROYAL MATRON

I. O.—Honored Marshal, present the Royal Matron-elect for installation.

MAR.—Royal Patron, it is with pleasure that I present Honored Lady .... who has been elected Royal Matron of this Court for the ensuing year.

I. O.—Honored Lady ...., I congratulate you upon your election to the highest position in the power of your associates to bestow. Their action in selecting you to preside over the deliberations of the Court is a guarantee of their confidence in your ability, and a proof of their respect and esteem. Previous to your investiture, it is necessary that you assent to the following pledges.

1. You admit that a belief in the existence of a Supreme Being is absolutely necessary to membership in the Order.

2. You promise to be just and equitable in your dealings while presiding over the Court.

3. You admit that the Chapter Order of the Eastern Star is the basis of the Adoptive Rite, and

that the name, character, and mode of recognition of the Order are unchangeable.

4. You promise to protect and obey the laws and regulations of the Supreme Council, the Grand Court, and the edicts of the Royal Grand Matron, and to permit no violation of them by the members of your Court.

5. You agree that the ceremonies of advancement can in no case be conferred, unless a Master Mason, in good standing, presides.

6. You admit that no new Court shall be formed without permission of the Grand Court, or Grand Royal Matron; and that no countenance be given to any illegally formed Court, its members, or persons initiated therein.

7. You agree that no visitor shall be received into your Court without due examination, nor when such visitor is likely to disturb the peace and harmony thereof.

8. You agree that no person can be regularly advanced in, or admitted a member of a Court, without previous notice, and proper investigation as to character.

9. You agree to promote the welfare of this Order, and will use your utmost endeavors to make yourself useful and your station honorable.

Do you promise to support and maintain these rules and regulations, and to enforce their observance by the members of your Court?

ANS.—I do.

I. O.—Face the West. Members of ....
Court, No. ...., you have heard your Sister-elect
in the sacred pledges she has made; are you satisfied, and do you promise to support her in the performance of her duties?

ANS.—We do.

(*R. Matron-elect faces East.*)

I. O.—The duties that will devolve upon you in
the important station to which you have been
elected, are of such a nature as to require the exercise of your utmost skill and ability as a presiding
officer. Think not that the field of intellectual service in this department has been so thoroughly
gleaned that there is nothing for you to gather.

You are to arouse the indolent, encourage the
despondent, and incite the unreflecting members of
the Court to activity, the influence whereof shall
be felt beyond its limits. As you are now devoted
to the cause of charity, sustained by truth, and
actuated by benevolence, your life will be sanctified
by deeds of love and kindness. Thus inspired, success will crown your efforts.

The objects of the Institution should never suffer
for want of intelligence on the part of its officers.
You will, therefore, perceive the necessity of pos-
sessing such qualifications as will enable you to
accomplish those duties which are incumbent upon

you in your responsible station. Your good example will remain as the best and highest lesson for your successors, showing them how to walk, and how to act to deserve well of the Order, to be entitled to its gratitude, and to win for themselves honor and reputation. You will now be invested with the jewel of your office. (*Done*)

Your badge is a Sword surmounted by a Crown, emblems of authority and dignity, admonishing you, that upon your judgment and discretion rest the government of this Court, and, in a great measure, the prosperity of our Order.

You will be conducted to the throne at my right hand.

ROYAL PATRON

I. O.—Honored Marshal, present the Royal Patron-elect for installation.

MAR.—Royal Patron, I have the honor of presenting Sir Knight ...., who has been elected Royal Patron of this Court, and now signifies his willingness to be installed into that responsible position.

I. O.—Sir Knight, you have heard the pledge made by the Royal Matron. Do you also promise a faithful obedience to all those regulations?

ANS.—I do.

I. O.—The station to which you have been elected is the most exalted within the power of the members of this Court to bestow upon a brother. You are to have a watchful care over the interests of the Court; to see that the laws of the Order are faithfully and promptly obeyed, and act as the constitutional adviser of the Royal Matron. Your specific duties in this organization are to preside at the election and installation of the officers, to assist at the advancement of candidates, and at such other times as required by the Royal Matron. Your well-known zeal in our cause induces me to believe that you will discharge these important duties with lasting benefit to the Court and honor to yourself.

Honored Marshal, invest the Sir Knight with the jewel of his office. (*Done*) Your badge is the Balance and the Fasces, surmounted by an antique lamp, lighted—emblems of authority, power, and knowledge. ' You will be conducted to your station.

ASSOCIATE PATRON

Honored Marshal, present the Associate Patron-elect for installation.

MAR.—*Royal Patron, I have the honor of presenting Sir Knight* ...., *who has been elected Associated Patron of this Court, and is ready for installation.*

I. O.—*Sir Knight* ...., *by the suffrages of the members of this Court, you have been elected to the position of Associate Patron. In the absence of the Royal Patron you will assume his duties.*

You will now be invested with the jewel of your office, and conducted to your station in the West. (Done)

ASSOCIATE MATRON

I. O.—Honored Marshal, present the Honored Associate Matron-elect.

MAR.—Royal Patron, I have the honor of presenting Honored Lady ...., who has been elected Honored Associate Matron, and is ready for installation.

I. O.—Honored Associate Matron, the office to which you have been elected, though in rank and power is second to that of the Royal Matron, is of great importance to the welfare and dignity of the Court. You are the assistant to the Royal Matron, and in her absence will succeed to all the privileges and prerogatives of her office. You heard the pledges made by the Royal Matron, previous to her installation. Do you also promise a faithful obedience to all those regulations in her absence?

ANS.—I do.

I. O.—It is necessary that you should make yourself familiar with the duties of the office of the Royal Matron, so that you may fill it with credit to yourself and honor to the Court. You will now be invested with the jewel of your office. (*Done*) Your badge is the wreath, emblem of honor and preferment, admonishing you to be faithful to your trust and deserving of the confidence reposed in you. You will be conducted to your station in the West. (*Done*)

TREASURER

I. O.—Honored Marshal, present the Honored Treasurer-elect.

MAR.—Royal Patron, I have the honor of presenting Honored Lady (*or Sir Knight*) ...., who has been elected Honored Treasurer of this Court, and is now ready for installation.

I. O.—You have been elected to fill a responsible position: to receive and disburse the funds of the Court. Your election to this position of trust is an evidence of the confidence the members have in your uprightness and integrity. The money placed in your hands is a sacred trust, and may be required for the relief of the widow and orphan, whom God may at the most unexpected moment send as the objects of our bounty; therefore, be ever ready to fulfill the trust.

Honored Marshal, invest the Honored Treasurer with the jewel of her (*or his*) office. (*Done*) Your badge is the Crossed Keys, an emblem of security, and admonishes you to the strictest fidelity in the discharge of your duties. You will be conducted to your station in the Northeast. (*Done*)

SECRETARY

I. O.—Honored Marshal, present the Honored Secretary-elect.

MAR.—Royal Patron, I have the honor of presenting Honored Lady (*or Sir Knight*) ...., who has been elected Honored Secretary of this Court, for installation.

I. O.—You have been honored by election to the important office of Secretary. Your duties are of a business and clerical character, and are of the utmost importance to the Court. You must be punctual in attending the meetings of the Court. You should be the first in your place, and your duties will probably hold you the last to leave it. You are particularly charged with the duty of watching the proceedings of the Court, and making record of all things proper to be written. You are to keep the financial accounts between the Court and its members, collect the revenue and pay it over to the Treasurer, to prepare the annual reports, and perform such clerical duties as pertain to your office. A good Secretary is a blessing to any institution. Your good inclination to the Order,

I hope, will induce you to discharge your duties with fidelity, and thus merit the esteem and confidence of your companions.

Honored Marshal, invest the Honored Secretary with the jewel of her (*or his*) office. (*Done*) In investing you with your official jewel, the Crossed Pens, I am persuaded that they will make an enduring record to your praise and to the welfare of the Order. You will now be conducted to your station in the Southeast. (*Done*)

CONDUCTRESS AND ASSOCIATE CONDUCTRESS

I. O.—Honored Marshal, present the Honored Conductress-elect and Honored Associate Conductress-elect.

MAR.—Royal Patron, I present for installation Honored Lady ...., who has been elected Honored Conductress, and Honored Lady ...., who has been elected Honored Associate Conductress of this Court.

I. O.—Honored Lady ...., the office of Honored Conductress, to which you have been elected, is one of the most important in the gift of this body. It will devolve upon you to see that the hall is supplied with the proper furniture, the decorations appropriately arranged for the meetings of the Court and the reception of visitors. It is your special duty to introduce and conduct the novitiate. Upon the faithful performance of these duties the usefulness and harmony of the Court greatly depends. Be careful, therefore, that the impressions made upon the candidate at reception are favorable.

Honored Lady . . . ., you have been elected to the office of Honored Associate Conductress, a position alike respectable and useful. It is your province to give a hearty cooperation in assisting the Honored Conductress in all that pertains to her duty, and to comply with the orders of the Royal Matron. By virtue of your position, you are the first officer to interview the candidate and prepare her for entrance into the Court. Remember, then, that it greatly depends upon the manner in which you receive and prepare the candidate, whether the first impressions are pleasant and lasting.

Honored Marshal, invest the Honored Ladies with the jewels of their respective offices. (*Done*)

Honored Marshal and Sir Knight, conduct the Honored Ladies to their respective stations in the South and North. (*Done*)

WARDER

I. O.—Honored Marshal, present the Honored Warder.

MAR.—Royal Patron, I present Honored Lady ...., who has been appointed Honored Warder of this Court, for installation.

I. O.—The office to which you have been appointed is one of much responsibility. To you is delegated the care of the inner entrance to our meetings. It is your duty to announce all alarms made at the door under your charge to the Royal Matron, from whom you will receive proper instruction. Your watchful care will preserve the Court from intrusion. You will be invested with the jewel of your office, and conducted to your station. (*Done*)

HERALD

I. O.—Honored Marshal, present the Honored Herald.

MAR.—(*with the Standard*) Royal Patron, I present for installation Honored Lady ...., who has been appointed Honored Herald of this Court.

I. O.—The office which has been assigned to you is one of dignity. Upon the Standard Bearer all eyes are fixed. We solicit your regular attendance at our meetings, that the Standard of the Order may be properly displayed whenever the members assemble, and the light and glory that emanate from our symbols may animate every heart. Be vigilant to protect this sacred possession. In all ages the Standard has been the central point of rally; the emblem of valor, patriotism, honor, home ties, all that distinguishes the civilized from the barbarous. Thousands have fallen to sustain it as the emblem of the country, and their last sigh has been a prayer for its preservation. (*The Standard is delivered to the Herald.*) Honored

Marshal, invest the Honored Herald with the jewel of her office, and conduct her to her station. (*Done*)

MARSHALS IN THE EAST AND WEST

I. O.—Honored Marshal, present the Honored Marshals in the East and West.

MAR.—Royal Patron, I have the honor to present Honored Ladies ...., who have been appointed Honored Marshals in the East and West, for installation.

I. O.—Honored Lady ...., your duties as Honored Marshal in the East are of special dignity and responsibility. You are to display the Flag of our Country; to escort the Royal Matron when she shall leave the East; to assist in the formation of processions and tableaux, and perform such other duties as occasion may require.

Honored Lady ...., your duties as Honored Marshal in the West are to assist in the ceremonies of the degree; to escort the Honored Associate Matron when she shall leave the West; to assist in the formation of processions and tableaux, and perform such other duties as occasion may require.

You will be invested with the jewels of your offices. (*Done*) Honored Marshal and Sir Knight, conduct the Honored Marshals to their stations in the East and West, respectively. (*Done*)

CHAPLAIN

I. O.—*Honored Marshal, present the Honored Chaplain.*

MAR.—*Royal Patron, I present Honored Lady (or Sir Knight)........, who has been appointed Honored Chaplain of this Court.*

I. O.—*The office entrusted to your care is a sacred one. In the discharge of your duties you will be required to lead the devotional exercises of the ceremonies. The dignity of the Court will depend in large measure on the manner in which you render your work. You will be invested with the jewel of your office and conducted to your station.* (Done.)

TRUTH, FAITH, WISDOM, AND CHARITY

I. O.—Honored Marshal, present the Honored Ladies who have been appointed to represent the four characters of the central figure. (*Sir Knight assists with Banners*)

MAR.—Royal Patron, I have the pleasure of presenting Honored Lady ...., who has been selected to represent Truth; Honored Lady ...., Faith; Honored Lady ...., Wisdom; Honored Lady ...., Charity, for installation.

I. O.—Honored Ladies, you are so placed as to form the square of the Court, immediately surrounding the Altar. In this position you are to emphasize the moral, intellectual, symbolical, and philosophical teachings of the Order, as set forth in its Ritual. I congratulate you upon being selected for so important a work. Much of the honor and usefulness of the Order depend upon the fidelity with which your duties are performed. The duties assigned to you are broad and extensive enough to give scope to your utmost abilities, and I am confident that nothing will be wanting on your part to make them instructive and pleasing. You will be invested with your jewels of office, presented with your banners, and conducted to your proper stations.

(Sir Knight assists the Honored Marshal in conducting them to their stations, one escorting Truth and Faith, the other, Charity and Wisdom.)

SENTINEL

I. O.—Honored Marshal, present the Sentinel.

MAR.—Royal Patron, I present for installation Sir Knight . . . ., who has been appointed Sentinel of this Court.

I. O.—Sir Knight . . . ., you have been appointed to the responsible position of Sentinel of this Court. Your courtesy should always be beyond question. See to it that the avenue of approach be strictly guarded. It is your duty to prepare the Court room for its meetings. You should know the business of every one who remains in the anteroom. If they desire to visit, the fact should be made known to the Royal Matron in the proper way, so that, if known, they may be admitted; if not known, examined. You are to perform such other duties as may be required. You will be invested with the jewel of your office, and conducted to your station.

I. O.—Royal Matron, your associate officers are at their respective stations, and nothing remains but for you to assume your own. To your charge is confided the Charter of this Court. It is the authority by which the Court is held. The value of this instrument is such that a meeting of the Court cannot be recognized as legal if the Charter is absent. You will carefully preserve it, and in no case should it ever be out of your control, and, when your term of office expires, you will duly transmit it to your successor in office. The Constitutions of the Supreme Council, the Grand Court, and the By-laws of this Court, are also placed in your keeping. You will be held personally responsible for a proper obedience and enforcement of the laws and regulations therein. The Bible upon the Altar will remind you of your obligations, and that as you judge here below, so will you be judged hereafter, and is confided to your care.

I now present you this emblem of power and justice—the Gavel. (*Hands her the gavel.*) It is also your emblem of authority for the government of this Court, which you will rule with courtesy, impartiality, and firmness. One blow of this instrument calls the Court to order (*); two blows call up the officers, (** *officers rise*) and three blows the entire Court (*** *every one in the room rises*).

Royal Matron and Royal Patron, behold your members.

Members of the Court, behold your Royal Matron and Royal Patron.

(*The grand honors are given by the Court, the Lady Marshal leading in the ceremony.*)

I. O.—* (*Court is seated*)

(*The Installing Officer may deliver an address or read the following*):

Honored Ladies and Sir Knights, having selected and appointed your office bearers, who have been inducted into their several stations with appropriate ceremonies, you cannot be insensible to the obligations of respect and obedience you owe them. It would indeed be a sorry compliment to your intelligence and regard for the Order, could it be supposed that you would fail in rendering them, collectively and individually, the weight of your

influence in the discharge of the functions with
which you have officially invested them.   In one
sense they are but your agents; therefore, their success or failure will redound to your credit or blame,
as you, yourselves, shall prove ready to second their
lawful undertakings, and, by your prompt obedience, set an example of loyalty to the Constitution
they represent.   There is one great truth which we
must all recognize, that "no man liveth unto himself alone."

The history of this Order is a bright and open
page, undimmed by any record but such as befits
the gallant and true.   Unquestioning fealty to the
Constitution and edicts of our organization, a warm
and generous support of the office bearers chosen
to represent you before the world, and a strict adherence to the Constitution of the Supreme Council
and Grand Court, have thus far been its distinguish-
ing characteristics; and now it remains for you to
continue the record, and hand down to your successors the glorious renown acquired by your pred-
ecessors.

Honored Marshal, you will make proclamation.

*(The Installing Marshal is escorted to the East by
the assisting Sir Knight where she ascends the throne;
the Installing Officer hands her the gavel.   The assisting Sir Knight stands at the foot of the throne while
the Mar. makes the proclamation.   After she has given
one blow of the gavel and replaced it on the pedestal,*

he takes her arm, assists her from the throne and escorts her to a seat.)

MAR.—In the name and by authority of the Supreme Patron (*or Grand Patron*), I proclaim the officers of .... Court, No. ...., duly elected, appointed, and installed.   *

INSTALLATION OF THE OFFICERS OF A GRAND COURT

OFFICERS OF A GRAND COURT

Grand Royal Matron, Grand Royal Patron, Grand Associate Matron, Sir Knight Grand Associate Patron, Honored Grand Treasurer, Honored Grand Secretary, Honored Grand Chaplain, Honored Grand Conductress, Honored Grand Associate Conductress, Sir Knight Grand Marshal, Honored Grand Lecturer, Honored Grand Warder, Honored Grand Herald, Honored Lady Truth, Honored Lady Faith, Honored Lady Wisdom, Honored Lady Charity, Honored Grand Sentinel.

The Grand Royal Patron of the preceding year, or a Past Grand Royal Patron, will proceed to the duty of installing the officers elect into their respective stations.

(An officer of a Masonic Grand Lodge, or the Master of a Lodge, may perform this service, assisted by a Grand Marshal.)

The chairs remain occupied by the officers who, having served their time, are about to retire from office. The ceremony will be conducted in the following order:

INST. OFFICER—Honored Ladies and Sir Knights, I am now prepared to install into their respective stations the officers of this Grand Court. Sir Knight Grand Marshal, you will present the officers-elect at the Altar for installation.

(*The officers are arranged by the Grand Marshal in a semi-circle around the Altar, facing the East, the Grand Royal Patron on the right, the Grand Royal Matron next, and so on according to rank.*)

GR. MAR.—Grand Royal Patron, the Grand Officers-elect are in order before you, and await your pleasure.

INST. OFF.—Honored Ladies and Sir Knights, you here behold those whom you have elected officers to serve you for the ensuing year. If any member of this Grand Court is apprised of any just or sufficient reason why any of these officers should not be installed, let the objection be now made known.

(*No objection being made, he proceeds*):

I will now administer the obligation of office, which you will each repeat. *** (*Grand Court is called up.*)

I (*each giving full name*), do solemnly pledge my honor, in the presence of Almighty God and of this Grand Court of the Order of the Amaranth, that I will, to the best of my ability, faithfully and impartially perform all the duties incumbent on the office to which I have been selected; that I will conform to the constitution, laws, rules, and regulations of this Grand Court, and in every way within my power assist in extending the usefulness of the Institution.

(The officers may be seated on one side of the room convenient to be presented in succession.)

INST. OFF.—* *(Grand Court is called to order.)*

GRAND ROYAL PATRON

Sir Knight Grand Marshal, you will present the Grand Royal Patron.

GR. MAR.—Worthy Sir, I have the honor to present Sir Knight ...., who has been elected Grand Royal Patron of the Grand Court, Order of the Amaranth, of the State of ...., for the ensuing year, for installation.

INST. OFF.—Sir Knight, we most cordially congratulate you upon your election to this, the most distinguished and important office within the gift of your associates. The confidence displayed by this Grand Court in elevating you to supreme command, is an ample guarantee to the Order throughout this jurisdiction, of your wisdom and of your worth. You cannot, Sir, be otherwise than aware of the deep and solemn consequence of the duties you are now about to assume, or of the many cares

and perplexities which surround its exalted honors.
These difficulties will, I am confident, be alleviated
by the affectionate sympathy and active assistance
of your associates. You may occasionally encounter
stern opposition from without, from those who do
not or will not understand our purposes; but as the
most dangerous and insidious enemy to the perpetuity and harmony of our beloved Institution will
pale before you in the uprightness of your adminis-
tration of its affairs, we can have no fears of the
results.

We now, Sir, have the honor to invest you with
the jewel of your office (*the Marshal invests him
with the jewel*), and with the emblem of your control (*hands the gavel*), which in your hands should
never be sounded in vain, and welcome you to the
East of the Grand Court, Order of the Amaranth,
of the State of ......, and render you this, the
first act of homage due to you as Grand Royal
Patron.

(*Bows low, with hands crossed on the breast. The
Grand Court is called up. • • •*)

I now salute and proclaim you Grand Royal Patron of the Order of the Amaranth, of the State of
...... Honored Ladies and Sir Knights, behold
your Grand Royal Patron. Grand Royal Patron,
behold your Sisters and Brothers.

(The assembly will, under the direction of the Installing Officer, salute the Grand Royal Patron with the grand honors. The Grand Court is called to order and seated *.)

GRAND ROYAL MATRON

INST. OFF.—Sir Knight Grand Marshal, you will present the Grand Royal Matron-elect.

GR. MAR.—I have the honor to present Honored Lady ...., who has been elected Grand Royal Matron of this Grand Court, for the ensuing year, for installation.

INST. OFF.—Honored Lady ...., the office to which you have been elected, is one of high dignity, and is one of great importance, for in the absence of the Grand Royal Patron from the meetings of the Grand Court, or from the limits of its jurisdiction, you are, by the Constitution, invested with his powers and with authority to exercise his high prerogatives. In view of such emergencies, allow us to remind you of the duty devolving on you, to be thoroughly prepared to fill his distinguished position with honor to yourself and advantage to the Order.

With pleasure we invest you with the jewel of office, and proclaim you Grand Royal Matron of the Order of the Amaranth of the State of ....

(The Installing Officer calls up the Grand Court, *** *and the Grand Royal Matron is saluted in the same manner as the Grand Royal Patron.)*

You will be seated in your place, at the right of the Grand Royal Patron.

(The Gr. Marshal will present the Grand Associate Patron in the same words as the previous officers.)

GRAND ASSOCIATE PATRON

INST. OFF.—Sir Knight ...., by the suffrages of the members of this Grand Court, you have been elected to the position of Grand Associate Patron. Be assiduous in the performance of your duties, so that you will truly be a strength and support to the Grand Royal Patron. In the absence of your superior officers, you will assume supreme command. Your fitness for the discharge of such a trust undoubtedly led to your selection for the office by your companions, and it will be your duty, and, no doubt, a pleasure, so to act as to justify their confidence.

You will now be invested with the jewel of your office, and conducted to your station in the West.

(The Grand Marshal presents the other officers in the following order, and with appropriate words.)

GRAND ASSOCIATE MATRON

INST. OFF.—Honored Lady ...., your associates have shown their confidence in your fidelity by electing you to the responsible position of Grand Associate Matron. Your previous devotion to the duties of the Order of the Amaranth is a sufficient guarantee that you will be a vigilant officer in whatever station you may be placed. It affords us much pleasure to have you invested with the jewel of your office.

You will be conducted to your station in the West, at the right of the Grand Associate Patron.

GRAND TREASURER

INST. OFF.—Honored Lady ...., your associates have been pleased to elect you to the responsible office of Treasurer of this Grand Court. Your integrity and truthfulness satisfy us that the trust is wisely reposed. It is your duty to receive all monies from the Grand Secretary; make due entry of the same, and pay them out on the order of the Grand Court, or Grand Patron, rendering accounts thereof. We are happy to have the privilege of investing you with the jewel of your office. The faithful performance of your duties will entitle you to the good opinion and thanks of your companions. You will be conducted to your station.

GRAND SECRETARY

INST. OFF.—Honored Lady ...., it is with extreme pleasure that we invest you with the jewel of your office. The duties of Grand Secretary are more varied, difficult, and I may add, pleasant, than those of any other officer in the Grand Court. Brought by your official position more immediately into communication with the whole body of the Order, it is requisite that you should possess ability, skill and industry, to meet the various demands upon you.

It is your duty to record all the proceedings of the Grand Court; to receive all monies due the Grand Court, and pay them over to the Grand Treasurer, and keep a just and true account of the same; to keep and affix the seal of the Grand Court to all proper documents, and carefully to preserve its archives. These are very important duties, on which, in a great measure, the usefulness of the Grand Court depends. Accuracy and punctuality are qualities which your office particularly requires; and as there is no place in the Grand Court in which a member can render more substantial service to the Order, I am confident that you will so perform its duties as to merit their esteem and receive their hearty approbation. You will be con-ducted to your station.

GRAND CHAPLAIN

INST. OFF.—Sir Knight, the sacred position of Grand Chaplain has been entrusted to your care. In the discharge of your duties you will be required to lead the devotional exercises of the sessions of the Grand Court, and to perform the sacred functions of your holy calling at all our public ceremonies. The principles and precepts of our association are in strict accordance with the best teachings and maxims found in the inspired volume, which is the chart and text-book of your sacred mission. Teach us from its life-giving precepts; intercede for us with that Divine Majesty which it so fully reveals and unfolds to us; and inspire us by its lessons of infinite wisdom and truth.

The profession which you have chosen for your lot in life is the best guarantee that you will discharge the duties of your present appointment with steadfastness and perseverance in well-doing. It is eminently appropriate that an emblem of the sacred volume, which sheds its benignant rays upon the altar of every lawful assemblage of our Order, should be the jewel of your office, with which you will now be invested and then conducted to your proper station, at the left, in front of the Grand Royal Patron.

GRAND CONDUCTRESS

INST. OFF.—Honored Lady ...., you have been elected to the honorable post of Grand Conductress of this Grand Court, and will now be invested with the jewel of office. Upon you will devolve the duties of receiving and introducing visitors; acting as the messenger of the Grand Officers, and as a useful assistant to the Grand Marshal in the ceremonies of the Order. Thus, your official position becomes one of great value and importance to the comfort and good order of the Grand Court. Vigilance and zeal are necessary requisites of your office, and we are confident that you possess these qualifications. You will be conducted to your station in the South.

GRAND ASSOCIATE CONDUCTRESS

INST. OFF.—Honored Lady ...., you have been elected Grand Associate Conductress, and will now be invested with the jewel of office. Your duties will require you to devote your attention to the condition of the Grand Court; to see that everything is in readiness for the meetings of the body; to act as special messenger of the Grand Royal Patron and Grand Royal Matron, and to assist the Grand Marshal and Grand Conductress in the performance of their duties. You will now be conducted to your station in the North, and remember that the post of honor is the post of duty.

GRAND MARSHAL

INST. OFF.—Sir Knight ...., you have been appointed Grand Marshal of this Grand Court. The duties of your office require care, promptness and activity. You are to arrange all processions of the Grand Court; to make the proclamations of the installations of the Grand Officers, and at the institution of new Courts, under direction of the Grand Royal Patron. Skill and precision are essentially necessary to the faithful discharge of these duties. You will now be invested with the jewel of your office, and be conducted to your station at the right, in front of the Grand Royal Patron.

GRAND LECTURER

INST. OFF.—Sir Knight ...., you have been appointed the Grand Lecturer and the Custodian of the Ritual of the Order in this jurisdiction, and we now invest you with the jewel of your office. It is your duty to instruct the members of the Order in the proper performance of their duties; to communicate light and information to the uninformed; to preserve our Ritual from change and innovation; and, by your instructions to the members, to illustrate the genius and vindicate the principles of our Institution. Let it be your object, while inculcating upon the members of this Order a faithful regard for its obligations, to impress them with a favorable opinion of its moral design and intellectual tendency. You will be conducted to your station at the left, in front of the Grand Royal Patron.

GRAND WARDER

INST. OFF.—Honored Lady ...., you have been elected Grand Warder of this Grand Court, and we now invest you with the jewel of your office. Your position is one of trust and responsibility. It is your duty to announce the approach of visitors and strangers. In so doing, possess yourself of the necessary information to announce their rank and position properly. Be cautious and vigilant, that no improper person may gain admittance. Your station is inside, at the door of entrance, on the right of the Grand Associate Matron.

GRAND HERALD, GRAND LADY TRUTH, GRAND LADY FAITH, GRAND LADY WISDOM, AND GRAND LADY CHARITY

INST. OFF.—Honored Ladies, you have been appointed severally to the offices of Grand Herald, Grand Lady Truth, Grand Lady Faith, Grand Lady Wisdom, and Grand Lady Charity. You are required to assist the Grand Officers generally in the discharge of their duties, and in every way in your power aid in the promotion of the interests of the Grand Court and the success of the Order. During the opening ceremonies of the Grand Court you will proclaim those sublime lessons of purity and faithfulness as exemplified by the same characters in the subordinate Court. You will be invested with the jewels of your several offices, and conducted to your stations.

GRAND SENTINEL

INST. OFF.—Sir Knight ...., you have been appointed Grand Sentinel of the Grand Court. Our Institution is of a sacred character, and an irreparable injury might result from a negligent or careless discharge of your duty. Your office is one of great importance, and requires unremitting care and watchfulness. Your station is outside the door. We now invest you with the jewel of your office, and you will repair to your place, and there be in active discharge of your duties.

INST. OFF.—(** *All the officers are called up*) It has fallen to your lot to be elevated to the highest places in the gift of this Grand Court. On entering upon the responsible duties of your several offices the members of this Grand Body expect you to devote yourselves with energy and zeal to the work allotted you to do. I need not remind you of the solemn obligations you have entered into with us, and that on you will depend much of our prosperity, harmony and success. May you be guided in the discharge of your duties by the spirit of the principles set forth in the sublime teachings of our Order.

In the organization of our Society, it is necessary that some should rule and others serve. A wise ruler seeks to elevate those to whom he is indebted for the position he occupies, and as a stream cannot rise higher than its source, so a ruler cannot gain prominence and glory greater than that enjoyed by his subjects. Let it be your aim to rise in office, for in so doing you elevate the whole Institution, and bring glory and honor to our beloved Order.

*** (*Grand Court is called up.*)

Honored Ladies and Sir Knights, let us all remember that we have a personal interest as well as a personal duty in the welfare of our Order, and that in proportion to our energy and zeal will be our success and prosperity. Let us feel assured that in all branches of our Order the progress, zeal and good conduct of the *members* are modeled upon the fidelity of the *officers*, and so be animated by the highest sense of duty. Let me exhort you in the words of the great Apostle: "Do all things without murmurings and without disputings," that you may be without blame, without spot, the children of God, irreproachable, in the midst of a people depraved and perverse, amongst whom you shine as lights in the world, bearing to them the word of life; so that in the day of judgment we may all feel that we have not travailed in vain or vainly labored in the work of the Order of the Amaranth.

Sir Knight Grand Marshal, you will proclaim the officers of the Grand Court duly elected, appointed and installed.

(*Grand Marshal will then make proclamation from the throne*):

GR. MAR.:

By order of the Grand Royal Patron and by authority of the Grand Court, Order of the Amaranth of the State of ...., I proclaim its Grand Officers elected, appointed and duly installed, in ample form. *

CONSTITUTING AND DEDICATING
A COURT

When a Charter has been granted by the Supreme Council or Grand Court, and the time has arrived for the ceremony of Constituting and Dedicating the new Court, the members will assemble in their room, and be in order, without a formal opening.

When a Grand Royal Patron or his representative performs the ceremony, the officers of the Supreme Council or Grand Court will assemble in an adjoining room. The G. R. P. directs the G. Cond., accompanied by the G. Marshal, to inform the R. M.-elect of his readiness to constitute and dedicate the Court and install its officers, which order is performed. As the G. Cond. enters the room, the Court is called up, *** when she says:

G. COND.—Royal Matron, officers and members of ...... Court, No. ...., I am instructed by the Supreme Patron (*or Grand Royal Patron*) to inform you that the Supreme Council (*or Grand Court*), at its recent meeting, was pleased to grant you a Charter; that they are desirous to constitute, dedicate, and install the officers, for which purpose they are now met.

R. M.—Honored Grand Conductress, please inform the Supreme Patron (*or Grand Royal Patron*) that we are ready to receive him and his associate officers.

(The G. Cond. and G. M. retire, and repeat to the G. R. P. the response of the R. M.-elect. The G. R. P. says):

G. R. P.—The Court now convened is prepared to receive us.

A procession is then formed in the following order:

Grand Marshal,	Grand Herald, with
Grand Assoc. Conductress,	Standard,
	Grand Conductress,
Grand Treasurer,	Grand Secretary,
Grand Lecturer,	Honored Truth,
Honored Charity,	Honored Faith,
Honored Wisdom,	Grand Warder,
Grand Chaplain,	
Grand Associate Matron,	Grand Associate Patron,
Grand Royal Patron,	Grand Royal Matron.

They enter the room, passing to the right and left of the Altar, which brings the G. R. P. and G. R. M. to the center. The G. R. P. and G. R. M. are invited to the East, when the grand honors are given. The R. M. presents the gavel to the G. R. P., and says:

R. M.—Grand Royal Patron, in behalf of . . . . . . Court, I bid you, and those who accompany you, a hearty welcome. Your presence is especially acceptable, when you come bearing the glad tidings of your intention to constitute and dedicate us permanently into a Court of the degree of the Amaranth, with power to perform our part in the great work of charity, benevolence, and kindness, and we are willing to assume the duties and responsibilities which additional powers for good will impose on us.

G. R. P.—Royal Matron, we thank you and your associates for your cordial welcome and good wishes; and we cannot too much commend the sentiments you have expressed. We shall now proceed to constitute and dedicate your Court and install its officers.

(G. R. P. requests the officers of the new Court to vacate their places, which are to be occupied by the Grand officers of corresponding titles.

*The Court will be called to order. * The Grand Marshal will seat the officers of the new Court together, on one side of the hall, in order. The jewels will be collected and placed in readiness for use*

ODE

G. R. P.—* At the recent session of the Supreme Council (*or Grand Court*) a Charter was granted to the members of this Court, establishing and confirming them in the rights and privileges of a regularly constituted Court of the Royal and Exalted degree of the Amaranth, which the Grand Secretary will now read.

(After the reading of the Charter, the G. R. P. will say):

G. R. P.—Honored Ladies and Sir Knights, you have heard read the Charter granted to this Court. Do you accept it upon the conditions therein named?

ANSWER— . . . .

G. R. P.—Honored Ladies and Sir Knights, the duties and responsibilities which you now propose to assume are serious and important. We greatly rejoice at the organization of every new body of the Royal and Exalted degree of the Amaranth.

To be constituted a Court of the Royal and Exalted degree of the Amaranth, is for all to take upon themselves new duties, and to enter into closer relations of interdependence. To perform those duties well requires constant effort, and a watchfulness over yourselves that never sleeps. When you are invested with the powers guaranteed by the Charter of Constitution, you may so act as to win honor, or so as to incur disgrace. There should be a firm and fixed determination, and steady purpose of mind, on the part of each, that the labors of this Court shall be made interesting and instructive; that they shall not be confined to the mere ceremony of opening, closing, and conferring the degree, but shall be devoted to mutual instruction, to the cultivation of the social feelings and acts of kindness, and to the practice of an active and earnest beneficence.

With these views, but briefly expressing the mission and purposes of our association, we will now proceed with the services for which we have assembled. But first let us beseech our Heavenly Father to prosper this work and bless our labors with success. ***

PRAYER

GR. CHAP.—Almighty Father, Who art in heaven, we invoke Thy benediction upon the purposes of our present assembly. Let this Court be established to Thine honor; let its officers be endowed with wisdom to discern and fidelity to pursue its truest interests; let its members be ever mindful of the duty they owe to their God, the obedience they owe to their officers, the love they owe to their associate members, and the good-will they owe to all mankind. Let this Court be consecrated to Thy glory, and its members ever exemplify their love to God by their beneficence to Him.

G. R. P.—* Sir Knight Grand Marshal, let the members of the Court about to be constituted, with their officers-elect, form around the Altar.

(*The Grand Marshal will place all the members in the form of a circle around the Altar. When so arranged, the Grand Marshal will say*):

G. M.—Grand Royal Patron, the members of the new Court, now about to be constituted, are in order.

G. R. P.—***

(*G. R. P. and G. R. M. will step within the circle, and the G. R. M. will say*):

G. R. M.—Honored Ladies and Sir Knights, before the Grand Royal Patron proceeds to constitute and dedicate your Court, we will receive your pledges of fidelity. These are entirely consistent with your former pledges as members of the Order.

1. That you will bear true fealty and allegiance to the laws and regulations of the Supreme Council, (*Grand Court,*) and the By-laws of the Court of which you may be a member.

ANS.—I will.

2. That you will not be governed by personal animosities or prejudice in matters that relate to members of your body, or to other worthy members of the Order, or to sisters or brothers applying for admission into your Court.

ANS.—I will not.

3. That you will contribute, so far as may be in your power, to the general good of the Order, avoid disputes, quarrels, and evil speaking, and be kind and courteous to members of the society wherever you meet them.

ANS.—I will.

G. R. M.—Repeat then with me.

ALL—These are my sacred and solemn pledges, and I will truly and religiously keep them.

(*The G. R. P. continues the ceremony*):

G. R. P.—Almighty Father, Who art constantly manifesting Thyself to us by Thy works, receive graciously the profound homage that we pay to Thee, and permit us to consecrate to Thee this living temple which we are now about to constitute.

Take under Thy special protection all those who shall be lawfully appointed to rule therein, that they may religiously comply with all the obligations by them contracted toward Thee, and toward all to whom they are bound by the bonds of duty.

Cause it to be that those who constitute this Court shall have but one heart, but one soul, to love, honor and obey Thee, as Thy Infinite Beneficence requires; and to love each other as Thou lovest them.

Banish from this temple all evil passions, all prejudices, all intolerance. May we meet each other here, as the children of our Father, Whose beneficent hand reaches all His children, and leads them by the same path to the gates of eternity.

And when the hand on Time's dial points to the last hour of our earthly labors, and the powers of life go away from us, help us to pass through the valley of the shadow of death, and lead us to that home wherein are peace and happiness for those who love and honor Thee and keep Thy commandments.

DEDICATION

(The G. R. P. returns to the throne, and with hands extended, says):

G. R. P.—In the name of our Heavenly Father, unto Whom be all honor and glory forever, and under the auspices of the Supreme Council (*or Grand Court*) of the State of ...., Royal and Exalted degree of the Amaranth, I do pronounce and declare this Court to be duly constituted and dedicated in ample form, under the distinctive title of .... Court, No. ....., Order of the Amaranth, in accordance with the terms of its Charter. I consecrate it as a living temple to works of Honor and Beneficence; to the service of Truth, Virtue, and Harmony. May Peace, Unity, and Loving Kindness always reign in it. May it abundantly prosper, and all its undertakings be wise and good, and crowned with success.

(A strain of triumphant music may be played. The G. R. P. says):

G. R. P.—Attention! Honored Ladies and Sir Knights, give the grand honors.

(Which being done, the G. R. P. says):

G. R. P.—We are now ready to install the officers of this Court. *

The Court is called to order, and the installation of officers takes place.

If the Grand Officers retire before the Court is closed, they will do so in the same manner they entered.

BADGE OF THE DEGREE

ROYAL MATRONS AND ROYAL PATRONS ADMINISTRATIVE DEGREE

PUBLISHERS NOTE: Because of the many demands for an Administrative Degree to be used in the Amaranth Courts, the Prince Hall Grand Amaranth Court of Michigan and Jurisdiction (to whom we are indebted) compiled and adopted the following Degree which we believe will be welcomed by many other jurisdictions as well where the Amaranth Degree is worked as a separate degree. A separate syllabus covering the secret work is sold separately. Secret parts in the Degree are indicated by references .to (5), etc.

SHORT FORM OPENING

G. R. M.—Grand Honored Warder, you will instruct the Grand Honored Sentinel that we are engaged in the solemn ceremonies of opening the ADMINISTRATIVE COUNCIL, and direct him to permit no interruption while we are thus engaged.

(Warder obeys and reports)

G. R. M.—Grand H. Conductress, are all Honored Ladies entitled to be present?

G. H. COND.—All the Honored Ladies are entitled to be present, Grand Royal Matron.

G. R. M.—Grand Royal Patron, are all the Sir Knights entitled to be present?

G. R. P. *will ascertain if all Sir Knights have been obligated in the Degree and if necessary take their pledge.*

G. R. P.—All the Sir Knights are entitled to be present, Grand Royal Matron.

G. R. M.—Grand H. Conductress, you will attend at the altar.

G. H. C. goes to altar and opens Bible at the 31st Chapter of Proverbs, then resumes her station; she does not read the Scripture.

G. R. M.—The Grand Honored Chaplain will pray. *** (*calls up Council*)

All should assume attitude of prayer, same as in Grand Court. G. H. Chaplain proceeds to altar.

G. H. CHAPLAIN—Almighty and Merciful God, grant that because we meet together, life may grow greater for some who have contempt for it; simpler for some who are confused by it; happier for some who are tasting the bitterness of it; safer for some who are feeling the peril of it; more friendly for some who are feeling the loneliness of it; serener for some who are throbbing with fever of it; holier for some for whom life has lost all dignity, beauty and meaning. Through Jesus Christ, Our Lord. Amen.

G. R. M.—We will sing our opening hymn, *My Faith Looks Up to Thee.*

ALL—(*Sing*)

G. R. M.—I now declare this Administrative

Council duly opened. * Grand Honored Warder, you will inform the G. Honored Sentinel that the Council is now open.

(*Warder obeys and reports*)

G. R. M.—Grand Royal Patron, we are ready for the conferring of the Administrative Degree. (*Hands him the gavel*)

G. R. P—Grand Honored Secretary, you will read the names of the Candidates.

G. H. S.—(*Reads the names of Candidates*)

G. R. P.—Grand Honored Conductress, you will escort the Candidates to seats near the East.

(*Cond. does so and when all are seated, G. R. P. continues*)

G. R. P.—Honored Ladies and Sir Knights, it is my privilege to portray to you at this time, the ADMINISTRATIVE DEGREE of the Royal and Exalted Degree of the Amaranth. This degree is intended to inspire, to instruct, and to draw into closer bonds of official intimacy the Royal Matrons and Royal Patrons, those who are about to assume, or have assumed, these official offices to which their associates in the Subordinate Courts have elected them.

The RITE OF ADOPTION was never designed to be wholly embodied within the limits of *one* degree; but, like the great institution into whose fraternal organization it was intended to be *adopted,* it should teach its lessons step by step, each advancing ceremony to be higher and more instructive in principle and design. The addition of other and different ceremonies, with beautiful illustrations of Truth, Wisdom, Faith, and Charity, all lovely graces, certainly enhances the value of any association, and gives it the right to rank among the great institutions of the world. The RITE OF ADOPTION is designed to be a real and permanent institution.

The Grand Royal Matron will give explanatory remarks.

G. R. M.—The RITE OF ADOPTION consists of the following degrees:

1. The Eastern Star, the first or initiatory degree.
2. The Queen of the South, the second degree.
3. The Amaranth, the third degree.

The rituals of these degrees, together with the Royal Matrons and Royal Patrons Administrative Degree, have been prepared with great care. The high and noble principles inculcated in them appeal to the better instincts of the human mind.

The special purpose for introducing the Amaranth Degree in its revised and distinct form is to present to the members of the Eastern Star an ADVANCED and INDEPENDENT organization of the RITE OF ADOPTION, under the title of COURT, thereby intending to afford the best means for

exemplifying and appreciating the superior qualities and sublime thoughts inculcated by the previous degrees, and in proper manner, supplying a
brighter light for those who are desirous of obtaining additional knowledge of the methods of
conducting the ceremonials and parliamentary
rules of literary, social and secret associations.

G. R. P.—You will listen attentively to King
Lemuel's lessons of chastity and temperance and
the praise and properties of a good wife found in
Proverbs 31.

G. A. P.—"The words of King Lemuel, the
prophecy that his mother taught him. What, my
son? and what, the son of my womb? and what,
the son of my vows? Give not thy strength unto
women, nor thy ways to that which destroyeth
kings.

"It is not for kings, O Lemuel, it is not for kings
to drink wine; nor for princes strong drinks: Lest
they drink, and forget the law, and pervert the
judgment of any of the afflicted.

"Give strong drink unto him that is ready to
perish, and wine unto those what be of heavy
hearts. Let him drink, and forget his poverty, and
remember his misery no more.

"Open thy mouth for the dumb in the cause of
all such as are appointed to destruction. Open
thy mouth, judge righteously, and plead the cause
of the poor and needy."

TRUTH—"Who can find a virtuous woman? for her price is far above rubies. The heart of her husband doth safely trust in her, so that he shall have no need of spoil. She will do him good and not evil all the days of her life. She seeketh wool, and flax, and worketh willingly with her hands. She is like the merchants' ships; she bringeth her food from afar."

FAITH—"She riseth also while it is yet night, and giveth meat to her household, and a portion to her maidens. She considereth a field, and buyeth it; with the fruit of her hands she planteth a vineyard. She girdeth her loins with strength, and strengtheneth her arms. She perceiveth that her merchandise is good; her candle goeth not out by night. She layeth her hands to the spindle, and her hands hold the distaff. She stretcheth out her hand to the poor; yea, she reacheth forth her hands to the needy."

WISDOM—"She is not afraid of the snow for her household: for all her household are clothed with scarlet. She maketh herself coverings of tapestry; her clothing is silk and purple. Her husband is known in the gates, when he sitteth among the elders of the land. She maketh fine linen, and selleth it; and delivereth girdles unto the merchant. Strength and honor are her clothing; and she shall rejoice in time to come. She openeth her mouth with wisdom; and in her tongue is the law of kindness."

CHARITY—"She looketh well to the ways of her household, and eateth not the bread of idleness. Her children arise up, and call her blessed; her husband also, and he praiseth her. Many daughters have done virtuously, but thou excellest them all. Favor is deceitful, and beauty is vain; but a woman that feareth the Lord, she shall be praised. Give her of the fruit of her hands; and let her own works praise her in the gates."

G. H. A. M.—Our labors of duty and love will soon be ended. As the lightening writes its fiery path on the dark cloud and expires, so the race of mankind, walking amid the surrounding shades of mortality, glitters for a moment through the dark gloom, and then vanishes from our sight forever.

G. R. P.—Honored Ladies and Sir Knights, we need not remind you of the high honors attached to the offices of a Royal Matron and a Royal Patron, and the weighty and delicate responsibilities to the work pertaining to a Subordinate Court. You are expected to see that the laws of the Amaranth are properly obeyed by the Sir Knights and Honored Ladies. And that you will exemplify, by your conduct, the beautiful tenets of the Royal and Exalted Degree of the Amaranth.

Before the secrets of the ADMINISTRATIVE DE-GREE can be imparted to you, I shall require your solemn pledge of honor to this Administrative Council. *** (*calls up Council*)

Sister Honored Conductress, prepare the Candidates for the obligation. (5)

(*G. R. P. leads all in the Lord's Prayer*)

G. R. P.—You will give your name in full and repeat after me _____(6)_____

G. R. P.—* (*seats the Council*) I will, with the help of the Grand Honored Conductress, give you the signs and passes. You will listen closely, and remember the following: (7)

G. R. P.—To assume the offices and responsibilities of a Royal Matron and a Royal Patron, you should possess the virtue of COURAGE. You should have the courage to face the TRUTH and defend it at all times. Courage to have FAITH in God, and in your own ability when all others doubt you. Courage to execute WISDOM and UNDERSTANDING in all decisions that confront you. Courage to extend CHARITY to anyone in need as far as you are able.

If you can possess and execute these virtues, you will truly guide and direct your Court and members to success. You must be both large enough and small enough to accept criticism and ideas, and correct any mistakes you may make.

All of these virtues you must practice. Being proficient in your ritual is not enough. You must never practice partiality among your members. Always show your respect and love for all.

G. R. M.—Having completed the work of this Administrative Degree, we shall proceed to close. *** (*calls up Council*)

The Grand Honored Chaplain will pray.

G. H. CHAP.—(*goes to altar*) Come Holy Comforter, move the midnight out of our lives. Let your warm sweet love of tenderness take possession of our being; frame every troubled care. May not the enemy of our souls steal away our good impressions. So, Lord, help us to let our light shine for Thee always. Amen.

G. R. M.—Grand Honored Conductress, attend at the altar.

(*Cond. proceeds to altar, makes salutation, closes the Bible, and resumes her station*)

G. R. M.—Grand Honored Warder, notify the Grand Honored Sentinel that this Council is now closed.

(*Warder executes the command and reports*)

G. R. M.—Honored Ladies and Sir Knights, farewell. *

(*Council is closed.*)

Administrative Degree Committee:

H. L. Elizabeth Nolan, P. G. R. M.

H. L. Maizie E. Johnston, P. G. R. M.

S. K. Sims G. Reid, P. G. R. P.

H. L. Hazel E. Hattler, P. G. R. M.

S. K. Jimmie Fowler, P. G. R. P.

H. L. Agnes Bristol, P. Int'l G. M.

S. K. G. Bernell Williams, 33°, Chairman, Sr. P. G. R. P.

H. L. Kathleen Williams, G. H. Secretary

FORM OF CERTIFICATE FOR ADMINISTRATIVE DEGREE

This is to Certify that _____ has received the ADMINISTRATIVE DEGREE of the ORDER OF THE AMARANTH, having been elected on ___ 19__ to serve as Royal _____ in _____ Court No. __, Rite of Adoption, located at _____ and working under a Charter from the Grand Court of the State of _____, and that __he has been properly instructed in the powers, duties, and responsibilities of such office.

In Testimony Whereof we have granted this Certificate under the hand and seal of the following officers of competent jurisdiction of the ADMINISTRATIVE COUNCIL this ___ day of ___ 19__

Attest _____ _____

Secretary of _____ Court No. __ _____

*9 7 8 1 6 3 9 2 3 2 3 8 3 *